# JOIN THE
# **LONGEVITY REVOLUTION**

A Guide for Financial Advisors
and their Clients

# JOIN THE
# LONGEVITY REVOLUTION

## A Guide for Financial Advisors and their Clients

Bradley C. Jenson, CFP®

John M. Comer, CFP®

James V. Gambone, Ph.D.

Foreword by Joseph F. Coughlin, Ph.D., Director, MIT AgeLab

**Join the Longevity Revolution**
**A Guide for Financial Advisors and their Clients**

by Bradley C. Jenson, CFP®, John M. Comer, CFP®, and James V. Gambone, Ph.D.

Editor: Dr. Jill Jenson
Cover photograph: istock by Getty Images – Michal Sanca
Designer & author photographs: Wendy J. Johnson, www.ElderEye.com

Published by Longevity Revolution Press
4243 Charles Road, Duluth, MN 55803, USA
www.LongevityRevolutionPress.com

First Edition, 2022

---

Join the Longevity Revolution: A Guide for Financial Advisors and their Clients / by Bradley C. Jenson, CFP®, John M. Comer, CFP®, and James V. Gambone, Ph.D.
ISBN: 9798357789471 (alk. paper)
Library of Congress Control Number: 2022948262

---

Manufactured in the United States of America by the KDP Independent Publishing Platform.

# Contents

# Acknowledgments

The authors want to thank Dr. Joseph Coughlin, Director of the Massachusetts Institute of Technology (MIT) AgeLab, for writing the Foreword to this book. As a widely recognized thought leader in longevity, Dr. Coughlin's support is especially appreciated. Thanks also to Lucas Bryant Yoquinto at MIT for reviewing our manuscript.

We are grateful to our editor, Dr. Jill Jenson, Associate Professor of Writing Studies, University of Minnesota Duluth, whose skills greatly improved the readability of the text. Many thanks to Wendy Johnson, Elder Eye Press, for the layout and design of the book, including the front and back covers, and for bringing the book to print.

We also wish to acknowledge the presenters of the annual Longevity Leaders World Congresses in 2020 and 2021, some of whom wrote books that provided material for this project. Brad's 2021 experience at a Modern Elder Academy (MEA) workshop in El Pescadero, Baja California Sur, Mexico was also an important influence on this book, so thanks to MEA founders Chip Conley, Christine Sperber, and Jeff Hamaoui for leading this excellent workshop. In addition, Jonathan Ainsley, Longevity Advisor Training Program at InvestinU.me, provided valuable insights for us on the subject of flourishing longevity.

We also appreciate the thought leadership of Marit Peterson, Associate Director of the Minnesota Elder Justice Center; Jay Haapala, Associate State Director of AARP Minnesota; Jennifer Fox, former Director of Consumer Outreach and Community Relations at the Minnesota Commerce Department; and Dr. Marlene Stum, Professor of Family Social Science at the University of Minnesota Twin Cities, all of whom helped us define practical steps to overcoming obstacles as we age.

A big note of thanks goes to those who read the manuscript and then endorsed our book: Frank McAleer, CFP®, CIMA®,

Senior Vice President, Wealth Planning, Global Wealth Solutions at Raymond James; Lee Baker, CFP®, President of Apex Financial Services and President of AARP of Georgia; Elissa Buie, CFP®, President/CEO of Yeske Buie, Trustee of the Foundation for Financial Planning, and former National Chair of the Financial Planning Association; and Janet Stanzak, CFP®, Principal of Financial Empowerment, LLC and former National Chair of the Financial Planning Association.

Finally, we wish to thank those from Raymond James Longevity Planning for their interest in this project: again, Frank McAleer; Amanda Stahl, Director, Raymond James Longevity Planning; and Alaina Butler, Longevity Planning Consultant.

– Bradley C. Jenson, CFP®, John M. Comer, CFP®, and James V. Gambone, Ph.D.

## The Vision

As financial advisors, Brad and John want to take this opportunity to thank our coauthor Dr. James Gambone for his vision on this project and for including us in it. Jim is singularly responsible for giving this book its most appropriate title: *Join the Longevity Revolution*. The notion of longevity was not widely recognized when Jim wrote his 2000 book, *ReFirement®: A Boomer's Guide to Life After 50*, about which Norma Schuh wrote, "This book offers a vision for elevating elderhood to its rightful place of respect, compassion, and celebration." Likewise, we hope and believe that Jim's vision for joining the Longevity Revolution will elevate the "modern elderhood" of all readers who read this new book and complete a longevity plan for themselves.

Thanks, Jim, for your vision and creativity.

– Brad and John

# Foreword

By Dr. Joseph F. Coughlin
Founder and Director of the MIT AgeLab
Author of *The Longevity Economy*

## "A Sea Change"

Old age isn't what it used to be—just ask anyone in the middle of it.

According to the mythical narrative handed down to us by our forebears, when we grow "old"—your definition of the term may vary—we become two things: greedy and needy. Greedy: for the simple pleasures enumerated in brochures for cruises and retirement living. And needy: for assistance when we're no longer able to provide for ourselves—be it economic, health related, or in our daily lives.

I wrote about these myths in 2017, in my book *The Longevity Economy*. (And to the paired notions "needy" and "greedy" I now sometimes add a third: "equally speedy"—the false idea that the same stages of aging arrive for everyone at roughly the same moment in our lives.)

These stereotypes—informed by medical missteps from the nineteenth century and frozen in place by institutions constructed at the dawn of the twentieth century—constrained the lived experience of old age for generations. This limiting force acted on financial planning, too, for the simple fact that it made old age seem like a solvable problem. If you knew your general biological trajectory and your needs (some combination of simple pleasures and basic requirements for life), then planning for old age amounted to little more than a math equation.

But the true complexity of old age couldn't stay hidden. It was always visible to anyone who cared to look: in the volunteerism, care responsibilities, personal and professional ambitions, and creativity of "older adults"—a set consisting of a maximally diverse group of people, accounting for every conceivable variation of race, belief, sexuality, and personality. (In fact, the set of "older people" can even be considered *age* diverse, since it potentially incorporates 60 or more years of human existence.) Complexity was there, too, in the diversity of their needs, which, though every bit as real as the needy/greedy stereotype suggested, were far more individuated. These crossed not one gamut but many, ranging from matters of health to those of the spirit, legal and financial guidance; it even worked its way into products and the built environment. Creating a world worthy of our older generations was never just a matter of providing enough money and health care—as crucial as these concerns continue to be—but also building desirability and accessibility into everything we touch, at any age, every day.

Happily, the number of people who recognize this complexity has grown markedly of late. In the financial advisory industry in particular, it would be fair to say that a sea change is taking place.

Part of this change has arisen from necessity. To the extent that the financial advice of yore revolved around mathematical computations, it was vulnerable to disruption from computer algorithms that could do the same work, essentially for free.

Financial advisors could—and do—offer far more value to their clients, however. The key involves setting aside our inherited, oversimplified myths around aging and tackling the true complexity involved in planning for the best possible later life. In so doing, the purview of planning ceases to be purely financial. "Longevity planning," in my preferred term, is substantially more holistic than financial planning, encompassing far more than the wealth needed for a generic older person to maintain base-level needs and simple pleasures. Its considerations cross a number of intersecting axes, including wealth, yes, but also clients' needs regarding transportation and help with household tasks; their idiosyncratic passions, goals, and social needs; their capacity for personal growth; and the extremely wide range of health contingencies that they and their loved ones may experience in the decades ahead.

To add still more complexity, such concerns interact in complex ways. Take health and isolation, for instance. An individual's health benefits from warding off loneliness, but making friends and socializing purely for the sake of improved health can feel backward, and older adults may reject programs built on this medicalized premise. Instead of pursuing relationships with the goal of maintaining one's health, it may make more sense to put the horse in front of the cart and treat health not as an end in itself, but rather instrumental to the goal of spending more time with the people we appreciate most. (That those relationships seem to boomerang back around and give a boost to health is, of course, a welcome bonus.)

For intersecting concerns ranging from dementia to dependents, legacy to extreme longevity, planning becomes a Rubik's Cube of sorts, where every move affects another facet of life.

A flowering of concerted inquiry into such matters has taken place in the past several decades, the findings of which have made their way into a cottage industry of books challenging old assumptions about aging. Individually, these are worth the time of anyone hoping to build a better old age for themselves or others, but, taken collectively, the stack (a pile I'm as responsible for as anyone!) has grown daunting.

Between the complexity now on the table in planning sessions and the sheer volume of literature available to longevity advisors and their clients, the demands on the time and attention of both parties have long since eclipsed most people's capacity to keep up. What's been needed for some time is a wide-ranging overview of new developments in longevity planning that offers advisors and clients alike on-ramps to areas of further interest.

The volume ahead, *Join the Longevity Revolution*, serves as that map: acting at once as the means for individuals to plot a path in their individual longevity planning, as well as a chart through the recent waves of literature applying new ideas to old age.

The text you will encounter in the pages to come will challenge received wisdom about longevity and impart wisdom of its own. One notion it takes on is the primacy of Abraham Maslow's pyramid of needs: the idea that basic, health-and-safety needs must be satisfied before all other concerns. The authors prefer instead the image of a sailboat, in which the fulfillment of fundamental needs and higher-order concerns, such as personal growth, proceed in concert toward a better, later life. As you embark on your own longevity journey—as client or advisor—may the words ahead help fill your sails.

# A Note to Clients

from Bradley Jenson, John Comer, and James Gambone

A bowhead whale can live for 200 years. An Aldabra giant tortoise can live for 250 years. An Antarctic sponge can live for 1,500 years. How about you? How long can you live? Not *that* long, to be sure, but perhaps longer than you think. To estimate your expected lifespan, you might be thinking about how long your parents or grandparents lived or about current longevity averages for women and men. But that's old-school thinking. With advances in medical biotechnology, if you have or develop good habits in diet, exercise, and other aspects of self-care, you can realistically think about living far beyond the current projections for longevity. As far back as the 1970s, science fiction writer Isaac Asimov suggested that humans had a maximum life expectancy of 115 years. Science is catching up with fiction. Living to be 100 or older is now a realistic possibility for many more people.

You might be thinking, "Who wants to be *that* old?" Well, there's good news! It's likely that you will extend *healthy* years of living rather than extending years of frailty or infirmity. And the vision for the 100-year life is a vision that more and more people are embracing. Ken Dychtwald's Age Wave, together with the Harris Poll and Edward Jones, asked Americans across five generations whether they wanted to live to age 100. A resounding 70 percent of Americans said, "yes"! Dychtwald concluded that the "yes" answer was contingent on staying healthy, engaged, and purposeful, which certainly makes sense.[1] How about you? Are you among the 70 percent of aspiring centenarians? If so, congratulations! You already have a vision for joining the Longevity Revolution.

But what, exactly, is the "Longevity Revolution"? First, it is a *scientific* revolution based on medical advances that will be coming fast and furious over the next decade, leading many, many more people to the 100+year life. Second, it is a *cultural* revolution because these scientific advances call for deep reflection on each individual's (a) purpose and passion for living (and, likely, working) for a much longer time, (b) core values for security and personal growth, (c) health habits for supporting the coming scientific advances, and (d) capacity to advance intergenerational relationships for a more fulfilling, longer life. Finally, it is a *financial* revolution because living healthier for longer necessarily requires more financial resources.

Indeed, this potential leap in longevity has huge implications for your future and thinking about retirement. The goal is that you flourish, living happily for more years than you ever dreamed possible. This is your opportunity to refire the next phase of your life with passion and purpose so that this leap in longevity results in a much more fulfilling future for you, for the people you love, and for the activities and causes you care about most. But how do you do that? Your greatest opportunity could very well be your greatest challenge.

The purpose of this book is to help you meet that challenge. It will teach you what the Longevity Revolution is and how you can prepare to join it. You will be inspired to see new possibilities for a longer, healthier life through notable research organizations and think tanks such as Age Wave, the London Business School, the Milken Institute's Center for the Future of Aging, the MIT AgeLab, the Stanford Center on Longevity, and others. We want to guide you through this new information so that you can create a plan to match your longevity potential. To help you accomplish this new envisioning process, there are questions at the end of each chapter for you to reflect on and, if you have a spouse or partner, to discuss your answers with. We strongly encourage you to keep a journal of your reflections as you move through this book, particularly in response to the Questions and Suggested Activities section at the end of each chapter.

The last chapter in the book, "Completing Your Personal Longevity Plan," is where the work that you have done at the end of each chapter is brought into an integrated whole. Like an artist working on a drawing, you will be able to sketch your future life in some detail, albeit with flexibility and individuality. Couples will create a longevity plan individually, but also together, as they adjust or blend personal goals to support both their relationship and their growth as individuals. The result will be a plan that allows you to live your life with passion and intentionality—to live life to the fullest in these wonderful years ahead of you.

After completing your longevity plan, you can then take a summary of your plan to your financial advisor, who will help you design a financial strategy for funding your leap in longevity. Of course, there is no guarantee that you will live to be 100 or more years, but we strongly encourage you to plan for what the research is showing you can realistically hope for and expect. It's your life to design, so why plan for a short life? Aim long and aim healthy!

In fact, as the authors of this book, we are "aiming long and healthy" ourselves. We hope you understand the authenticity and genuine passion we have for helping you see and seize the possibilities of the Longevity Revolution for your life. The only thing that can possibly stop you from succeeding in this venture is your attitude. Can you or can't you adopt the necessary positive attitude for effective longevity planning? As the old saying goes, "Whether you think you can, or you think you can't—you're right." With the right attitude, you *can* refire your life for healthy longevity. **Welcome to the Longevity Revolution!**

# A Note to Financial Advisors

from Bradley Jenson

"I'm in a rut. I'm tired of the same old routine. I'm sick of the inflexibility. I don't have enough free time. I've lost my spark. I'm just burned out." How many times have you heard such comments from clients in their late fifties or early sixties who come to talk to you about retiring? All they can think about is quitting their "day job."

Early in my career as a financial advisor, I attended an event where I heard Dr. James Gambone deliver a powerful message: "Don't retire. ReFire!" In his book *ReFirement®: A Boomer's Guide to Life After 50,* published in 2000, he foresaw that the "Boomer" generation would both want and need to redefine what the retirement years meant. He suggested a new paradigm to replace retirement, choosing the most appropriate symbol—fire. For centuries fire has been associated with life, health, and renewed spiritual energy. The message resonated with me because I was approaching my fifties and in need of "refiring" my own vocational life. My career change from pastoral ministry to financial services gave me a new sense of purpose in helping people make informed decisions about their money and their future. My "fire" was the challenge of a new career and the intellectual task of becoming a CERTIFIED FINANCIAL PLANNER™ professional.

Now, more than 20 years after *ReFirement®* was first published, the concept of "refiring one's life" is more relevant than ever. The trailing edge of the Boomer generation is in their late 50s and coming advances in biotechnology will make being healthy and fit through one's 90s to the 100+year life a realistic possibility for more and more people.

To be sure, not everyone will live to be 100 years old, but many, if not most, should plan on it. Why? There is currently a gap of about 15 to 20 years between people's vision of their vital years and the future possibility that they may experience. People tend to think they will "peter out" sometime in their 80s, if not before, but what if they don't? What if they have another 15 to 20 years of healthy living *after* they hit age 85? If so, two essential elements will likely be missing from their original financial planning process. First, they will need a vision for what they will do for two (or more) decades longer than they thought they would live. Second, they will need a financial plan and an investment strategy that stretches to their 100th year or beyond.

This is why Jim decided to do a complete re-write of *ReFirement*®. He sought to combine the vision for refiring one's life with the best current research on aging. After he and I became reacquainted in 2018, I was delighted that he asked me, as a CERTIFIED FINANCIAL PLANNER™ professional, to co-author this new book. John Comer, also a CERTIFIED FINANCIAL PLANNER™ professional, joined the team in 2019.

The result is the book you are holding, *Join the Longevity Revolution: A Guide for Financial Advisors and Their Clients*. It not only has a new name but a new audience: those who want to be part of the Longevity Revolution. We believe it's vital for financial advisors and their clients to embrace the vision of a potential leap in healthy longevity and plan for it. The book will also enhance advisor–client relationships by providing Questions and Suggested Activities at the end of each chapter to prompt meaningful reflection and discussion regarding longevity concepts. The concepts, questions, answers, and discussions that take place between and with your clients are meant to be integrated into a Personal Longevity Plan. With this Personal Longevity Plan in hand, you can work with clients to implement financial strategies that meet clients' needs for a much longer, more fulfilling life.

As a financial advisor, you will have the privilege of watching clients live with refired vitality during this longer, healthier life. We hope that you, as advisors, also become inspired to create your own Personal Longevity Plan and refire right along with your clients. **Welcome to the Longevity Revolution!**

# Moving from Retirement Planning to Longevity Planning

**"We might want to start talking about longevity planning, rather than retirement planning."** – Joseph F. Coughlin, Massachusetts Institute of Technology (MIT) AgeLab

In order for you to grasp the importance of having a longevity plan rather than just a retirement plan, you must first believe that you have a realistic possibility of becoming a healthy, active centenarian. For most of you, that's probably something you currently do *not* believe. The purpose of this chapter is to help you become a believer, a believer in your potential for becoming a vigorous centenarian and a believer in the importance of creating a Personal Longevity Plan.

We hear about active centenarians today, but these people are considered exceptional, not commonplace. Consider Orville Rogers, who passed away just a couple of years ago. A World War II veteran who trained pilots during the war, he later became a commercial pilot who took up running in his 50s. As a centenarian, he was still running and setting records.[2] Then there's Tao Porchon-Lynch, a model and a cabaret dancer who started teaching yoga in her mid-60s—the same age most of you consider the age to retire. She was still teaching at the age of 100![3] If setting running records and teaching yoga at the age of 100 don't impress you, what about skydiving? In 2018, at the age of 102, Irene O'Shea of Australia became the world's oldest tandem skydiver. Of course, that record stood only until 2020, when 103-year-old Al Blaschke of Texas took a 14,000-foot skydiving plunge to celebrate his twin grandsons' college graduations. The "youngsters" decided to take the plunge along with grandpa.[4]

When we read or hear about such people, we smile and marvel at their accomplishments, but we rarely consider the possibility that we ourselves could eventually do the same thing and live as healthy, active centenarians. Why not? What prevents the average person from considering this a viable possibility? First, most of us are aware that the current average lifespan in the United States is way short of the century mark: age 76 for men and age 81 for women. If you have already reached age 65, you can add 10 years to these numbers, but that would still be well short of 100. Beyond our knowledge of national averages, however, is the fact that our personal expectations for longevity are typically rooted in our family of origin. In other words, we look at how long our parents and grandparents lived to estimate how long we will live. The problem with such thinking is that it does not take into account current scientific research and future discoveries concerning aging.

While a full overview of that kind of research is beyond the scope of this book, you do need at least a brief summary of today's state-of-the-art research involving geroscience and medical biotechnology that will extend healthy longevity, research that could very well affect your future. "Geroscience" is a relatively new term, so you may not have heard of it. According to the American Federation for Aging Research, geroscience is "a research paradigm based in addressing the biology of aging and [the] biology of age-related diseases together."[5] Similarly, medical biotechnology is a type of scientific research that uses living cells and cellular material to diagnose and treat diseases. We use the term "aging science" as a comprehensive term encompassing both geroscience and medical biotechnology. As you can imagine, this aging science is highly technical and can be hard to understand. At the same time, it is not necessary to have a deep understanding of this science—we don't—to believe that it will soon deliver a healthy 100+year life for many more people.

Few people want to live a longer life if they aren't also going to be healthy during that extended lifespan, so looking at both is important. Without "getting too deep into the weeds," what follows are a few examples of the work currently being done to extend not only your lifespan, but also your healthspan.

Let's start with some current research on aging. The Buck Institute in California conducts biomedical research to understand what aging actually is. Their researchers say, "We believe it is possible for people to enjoy their lives at 95 as much as they do at 25...."[6] The Institute is researching drugs that can slow the aging process, increase health, and extend life.

Important work is also being done to put an end to the harmful diseases we all know are associated with aging. For example, the drug company Alkahest targets neurodegenerative diseases, such as Alzheimer's, Parkinson's, and other inflammatory disorders. Since about one in five hundred people are affected with Parkinson's disease, and 5.8 million people in the U.S. alone have Alzheimer's, the research being done at Alkahest could positively affect millions of us!

Through the Institute for Aging Research, Albert Einstein College of Medicine, Nir Barzilai, M.D., has made a fascinating study of 750 Super Agers—individuals who maintain active lives well into their 90s and beyond. These Super Agers have reached their 90s without having experienced cardiovascular disease, cancer, diabetes, or cognitive decline. One might think that these people have healthier lifestyles than most people do, but they don't. Their genes are primarily responsible for their longevity.[7] Although most of us do not share the genes that deliver the 100+year life, future advances in gene editing may very well help us get there. In his book *Age Later*, Barzilai makes the important point that artificial intelligence is key to the speed at which aging science is developing. He writes, "One of the reasons we're able to make such great strides forward with research is that artificial intelligence allows us to process massive amounts of data."[8]

The aforementioned Buck Institute has also partnered with the famed Mayo Clinic to establish Unity Biotechnology, Inc., one of the first therapeutics companies focused on removing harmful senescence cells from the body. What, exactly, are senescence cells? Put quite simply, they are cells that have stopped dividing. Barzilai explains, "When cells divide for the last time, their appearance and functions change. . . . These [senescent] cells become more plentiful with age . . . ."[9] Whereas it can be good and necessary for senescence to occur to prevent the growth of damaged cells, such as cancer cells, the accumulation of senescent cells in tissues may cause inflammation and age-related diseases. Barzilai adds, "*Senolytics* is the name of a group of drugs that [researchers] . . . are trying to develop to decrease the number of [senescent] cells."[10] In other words, such drugs would lower the number of senescent cells in your body, thereby increasing both your healthspan and lifespan.

These examples represent just a few of the hundreds like them from around the world, all aimed at discovering ways to extend human healthspan as well as lifespan. At this point, you're probably thinking this sort of research is interesting but likely more science fiction than reality, at least in your lifetime. Just how long is it going to take for this 100+ healthy life to materialize?

A 2019 *Forbes* article quoted Greg Baily, M.D., of the biotech company Juvenescence, who said, "Science fiction is becoming science." To help illustrate the speed at which aging science is advancing, Baily gave the following illustration: "'In 1903, two brothers flew a glorified kite for 14 seconds, the Kitty Hawk. Fifteen years later they were flying planes in WWI, and 35 years later, the Germans had invented the jet. Sixty-five years later we landed a man on the moon. For robotics and for aging, divide that number by 10. That's how fast this is going to happen.'"[11] Using Baily's comparison and simple math, if it took 65 years from the Wright brothers' first flight to landing on the moon, and if with the current state of science and technology we can divide that number by 10, then we can conclude that the leap in healthy longevity could happen by 2030. Put in a slightly different way, Michael Roizen, M.D., Chief Wellness Officer Emeritus at the Cleveland Clinic, has said that by 2030, 90 will be the new 40![12] The next decade is simply not that far away.

How old will you be in another eight years or so? Maybe 65? 75? 85? Unless you have already lived into what we now know as "old age," you are probably going to see the fruits of the research into healthy 100+year living in your lifetime, and you, too, will be able to take advantage of the benefits this type of scientific discovery has to offer. In their book *The 100-Year Life: Living and Working in the Age of Longevity*, Dr. Lynda Gratton and Dr. Andrew Scott of the London Business School write, ". . . you would be wise not to simply think of living healthily for 100 years, but rather consider this the very minimum you can expect."[13]

If you still aren't quite convinced and need a more recent, real-life example of the speed of scientific research, consider the astonishing speed with which the first two COVID-19 vaccinations were developed. When most of the world was in lockdown in March 2020, the notion that a safe and efficacious vaccine could be developed in less than nine months seemed laughable, even to many doctors and infectious disease experts. But then it happened. Another example of the speed of scientific discovery is found in Walter Isaacson's 2021 in-depth book *The Code Breaker: Jennifer Doudna, Gene Editing, and the Future of the Human Race*. Reading this book, you find that life in a 21st-century science lab is anything but plodding along. On the contrary, we are living in a world that has brilliant scientists doing cutting-edge research and using state-of-the-art technology at a sprinter's pace. What this means is that even for those who are currently 65 and live a healthy life into their mid-80s, science would have two decades to create the leap in longevity these authors and researchers are predicting. Needless to say, life does not come with guarantees, but all signs point to the "leap in longevity" forecast becoming a reality sooner than we imagine.

# Longevity: The New Frontier in Financial Planning

Now that you know what the future holds and the speed at which that future is going to arrive, how are you going to respond? You have only two options. The first is to continue planning the rest of your life based on current industry standards for lifespan averages and the number of years your parents and grandparents lived. The second and far more exciting option is to embrace the very real possibility that you will live a long, healthy life and plan accordingly.

If you go with the first option, you will likely participate in traditional retirement planning, which focuses on three main questions:

1. How old do you want to be when you quit working?

2. How much money do you need to fund your retirement lifestyle?

3. How long do you think you might live?

To help create this sort of plan, a major financial services firm set the default in their financial planning software at a 90-year lifespan for men and a 93-year lifespan for women—much higher than the current U.S. averages of 76 for men and 81 for women mentioned earlier. The rationale for doing this was to ensure that their clients didn't run short of money before they died, obviously a wise thing to do. As mentioned previously, most people still anchor their longevity expectations to either these current averages or their family history. This type of planning begs the question: What if you were to live to age 100 or more, experiencing more than two decades of lifespan beyond the current averages? Having a financial plan that extends *only* to age 90 or so might be a significant problem for you. The potential of needing financial resources for 10 years or more beyond what was originally planned could lead to a significant funding gap. In short, you might have a lot of life left at the end of your money.

This is why Dr. Joseph Coughlin of the MIT AgeLab advises that longevity planning should replace traditional retirement planning. We refer to this second option as having a plan for joining the Longevity Revolution, which leads to creating your Personal Longevity Plan. Indeed, the Longevity Revolution launches us into a new frontier in financial planning. Financial advisors who catch the vision for the Longevity Revolution and become early adopters of longevity planning will develop longevity coaching skills to help clients move into this new frontier. The specifics of such longevity planning will be discussed later, but for now, we want to help all those involved in financial planning, clients and financial advisors alike, to begin thinking anew about their future in three major areas of life: work, education, and home.

# Re-envisioning Work, Education, and Home for the Longevity Revolution

## Work

Let's begin with our work life. For better or worse, active living into a 10th or 11th decade likely involves working much later in life than did our parents or grandparents. As Lynda Gratton said, "When we live longer, the three-stage life of full-time education, full-time work, and full-time retirement looks ridiculous."[14] This three-stage life with full-time retirement beginning in one's 60s may have worked well for our parents and grandparents, but it is quickly losing its relevance and viability in the Longevity

Revolution. Again, from Gratton, "If we live to be 100, we're going to be working until we're 70 or 80."[15] Perhaps not everybody, especially if people have enough financial resources to fund the 100+year life, but for most people, it will likely be true that they will be working for income much later in life than previously expected.

Even if they have adequate financial resources to fund a very long life, retirement in one's early 60s will probably not be a good idea for people who live to be centenarians. Our overall well-being and happiness usually require the kind of cognitive stimulation, emotional vitality, and social interaction that work can provide. To be sure, working much later in life doesn't necessarily mean staying in your current position or field, nor does it mean that you will necessarily have to work full-time. In a best-case scenario, working later in life would involve doing interesting work with interesting people on a schedule of your choosing. Such circumstances supply the stimulation and vitality most people crave at any age.

If the thought of starting over after a long career concerns you, you've already seen it done really well, way before the Longevity Revolution. Although you probably don't know Anna Mary Robertson Moses, you do know "Grandma Moses," the famous painter. Born before the Civil War, she *began* her professional and highly successful painting career at age 78, dying at the age of 101 in 1961. Could it be that her passion for working on something new late in life contributed to her vitality and longevity? Likely so.

## Education

Lifelong learning is already well-established in the culture. After retirement such learning falls into the realm of leisure pursuits, things done totally because you want to do them, not because you have to do them. This type of lifelong learning covers a broad category that involves everything from "university for seniors" courses (opportunities created by a local college or university) to community education programs to book clubs to Road Scholar trips. The possibilities are endless. Lifelong learning in the Longevity Revolution retains these different venues and the variety of subject matter.

What will change in the Longevity Revolution is an increased focus on work-related lifelong learning as a matter of necessity, not leisure. Because most people will be working later in life, they will also be learning as a part of their employment. Work-related lifelong learning is for knowledge accumulation related to up-skilling a current job or re-skilling a different one. Both up-skilling and re-skilling are often related to improvements in technology, which never stands still. In the decades to come, elders in the Longevity Revolution will be re-skilling for jobs that don't even exist yet. In a world of increased use of robotics and other forms of artificial intelligence, interesting jobs in tomorrow's economy are going to require even more knowledge and technological skills than they do today. Work-related lifelong learning will simply be a part of life in the Longevity Revolution.

In addition to lifelong learning, another type of education—long-life learning—will play an integral role in the Longevity Revolution. Long-life learning, as opposed to lifelong learning, is much more than a rearrangement of adjectives. A fairly recent phenomenon still in the early stages of impacting the culture, long-life learning will become essential for joining the Longevity Revolution. But what is it?

Chip Conley, co-founder of the Modern Elder Academy, and Dr. Ingo Rauth highlight four distinguishing features of long-life learning, which we list below, along with the ways in which this book addresses each:

1. **Personal well-being and fulfillment, which includes developing a growth mindset and the ability to effectively navigate life transitions**

   Our book addresses this aspect of long-life learning through a discussion of core values, including a growth mindset, for the Longevity Revolution (see Chapter 3).

2. **The importance of purpose that extends into later life**

   We highlight the importance of clarifying and enhancing your life purpose in this chapter.

3. **Best practices for mid-life and beyond based on personal development theories**

   This book emphasizes the concept of juvenescence (i.e., growing younger as you age), the development of wisdom, and the importance of goal setting for the Longevity Revolution (see Chapters 2, 8, and 9).

4. **Approaches to enhance intergenerational relationships**

   We devote Chapter 5 to the value of building intergenerational relationships for thriving in the Longevity Revolution.

In short, education in the Longevity Revolution will indeed involve both lifelong and long-life learning, but the more important of the two is long-life learning because these four distinguishing features are the keys that unlock the door to thriving, rather than just surviving, in the Longevity Revolution.

## Home

In addition to work and education, where we live out our later years will be rethought by many people. Paul Irving, J.D., founding chairman of the Milken Institute's Center for the Future of Aging, speculates, "We'll age in place—rejecting the model of an isolated life in a distant retirement community with a recreation center, a shuffleboard court, and a cafeteria. Instead, we'll continue, and even increase, active involvement in our communities, educational and arts institutions, civic and charitable organizations, businesses, and places of worship."[16] Aging in place makes sense for many because it allows building on current community relationships and staying close to places of employment. As such, aging in place may very well become the norm for those living in the Longevity Revolution. That being said, retirement communities aren't going away, and many people will choose to make that transition at some point, but the changes in our work and education choices as dictated by the Longevity Revolution may delay this type of move.

# Purpose and Passion for Living in the Longevity Revolution

One of the co-authors of this book, Dr. James Gambone, was an early visionary in longevity planning before it was even called longevity planning. It's been over 20 years since Jim's book *ReFirement*® was published, but even back then, he was encouraging us to refire our lives for healthy aging. Having this fire necessitates uncovering your purpose and passion for living well in this next phase of your life, the Longevity Revolution phase.

## Ikigai (pronounced EE-KEY-GUY): Life Purpose

In their book *Ikigai: The Japanese Secret to a Long and Happy Life*, Héctor García and Francesc Miralles quote a relevant Japanese proverb: "Only staying active will make you want to live a hundred years." How true! Whether or not you retire, as you grow older, it's important to refire your life by staying active. The question is active doing what? The answer is spending significant time on your ikigai, your purpose for living, your reason for getting up in the morning. Some people can immediately identify their purpose, while for others, doing so takes time and effort. Nevertheless, it is vital to do.

Richard Leider and David Shapiro apply the ikigai concept to longevity in their book *Who Do You Want to Be When You Grow Old?: The Path of Purposeful Aging*. They make the interesting point that while "[e]veryone is *getting old*; not everyone is *growing* old."[17] In other words, too often people retire and coast through the rest of their life without *growing* at all. Claiming and living by your ikigai prevents you from sleepwalking through the final phase of your life.

Almost all discussions of ikigai seem to presume that "purpose" is singular, that knowing your purpose means identifying one thing. Of course, it's fine if your purpose in life is singular, but we believe that you could have more than one purpose for living, maybe even several. If you do, you have what we call a "purpose portfolio."

## Passion

The words "purpose" and "passion" are often used interchangeably, but they are not quite the same. Perhaps one way to distinguish between the two is to say that passion is the degree to which you focus on your life's purpose(s). As such, your passion becomes your guide for the choices you make when setting goals for the Longevity Revolution. Your core values (discussed in Chapter 3) together with your passion and purpose(s) create a powerful combination for deciding what's important to you for a long, healthy, fulfilling life.

Lance Secretan's *The Spark, the Flame, and the Torch* makes this profound statement: "Passion is the authentic guide for our choices."[18] With respect to creating an excellent longevity plan for yourself, you must be clear on exactly what you are passionate about. Without that knowledge, you can't effectively answer the key longevity-planning question, **"How can I make my potential 100+year life the most fulfilling it can be?"** Put simply, passion is a prerequisite for effective longevity planning, and to discover your passion, you must find the spark, in Secretan's terms, that sets your passion on fire:

> The spark is essential for all of us to be inspired—it fires up the will. A spark must be present in order to initiate excitement, passion, a hunger of the spirit, an ambition to accomplish something special, to make a difference. The spark is a sudden awareness, a stirring within, an awakening of our potential, a growing enthusiasm . . . . The spark ignites the soul.[19]

Secretan suggests exploring your passion by asking one over-arching life question: "Why am I here?" That question alone encourages you to reflect deeply and to identify, or further clarify, the spark that ignites your soul and will engage you in your quest to live a fulfilling life in the Longevity Revolution.

Furthermore, becoming clear about your passion for living is directly correlated to your sense of personal happiness. Cassandra Gaisford, author of *Midlife Career Rescue: The Call for Change*, puts it simply: "All we need to make us really happy is something to be passionate about."[20] And if you think that passion is for somebody else but not you, think again. Gaisford writes:

> Every human being is capable of passion. But many people think they are not. Remember, different people are passionate in different ways. Many people think that being passionate only means being loud and extroverted. This isn't true at all. Passionate people come in all shapes, sizes, and ages. You can pursue your passion at any age and stage of your life.[21]

In other words, your passion and purpose(s) could be anything from family to career to special interests to something you have not yet explored or experienced. So go for it! Do whatever it takes to identify, clarify, and enhance your passion and purpose(s) for living the most fulfilling life you can possibly live as you *grow*, not just get, older.

To begin your intentional journey in the Longevity Revolution, we are asking you to complete the Questions and Suggested Activities at the end of each chapter in this book, and if you have a life partner, discuss your responses with that person. When you reach the last chapter, you will use what you wrote to complete your Personal Longevity Plan.

# Questions and Suggested Activities

To get the most value out of reading this book, it is necessary for you to start a **Longevity Planning Journal**. Whereas you could do this by making hand-written journal entries, it would be best if you download the Longevity Planning Journal document from our website, **LongevityRevolutionPress.com**, and record your responses there. That being said, use the method you prefer and that works best for you.

1 Think about longevity in your family of origin. To what age did your grandparents and parents live? If some are still living, describe their health and lifestyle.

2 Given the coming advances in aging science for healthspan as well as lifespan, how convinced are you that living to 100 and beyond is a distinct possibility for you? If you could be both old *and* healthy, to what age would you want to live? What year would that be?

**3** Imagine that you have many more years of healthy living ahead of you than your parents or grandparents had. In a paragraph or two, describe activities you would find enjoyable and meaningful during this time.

**4** Write about your passion and purpose(s) for living by considering these questions:

a. What is currently true for you in terms of your purpose and passion?

b. Do you have a singular purpose in life, one ikigai, or do you have a purpose portfolio? In either case, write about your purpose(s).

c. If you are pondering your purpose in life and seeking more clarity, you may want to ask this simple question: What "dulls" you and what "spirits" you? Then, make a list of the things you are doing in your life that dull you. Estimate how much time each day you spend on activities that dull you. Make a contrasting list of the things that truly spirit you and estimate how much time a day you spend on "spirit activities." The more time you can spend on activities that spirit you, the closer you are to your passion and purpose(s).

5 If you need more clarity, try taking The Purpose Exchange self-evaluation (thepurposexchange.com/self-evaluation). It takes less than 10 minutes, and it's free. When finished, reflect on what you learned.

# 2

# Understanding Juvenescence for Your Longevity Journey

**N**ow that you know the 100+year life is a real possibility and have started to explore what you might want to do with the potential of three decades (or more) of healthy living beyond age 65, the question becomes, **"How can I make my potential 100+year life the most fulfilling it can be?"** Now *that* is a great longevity planning question! To answer the question, however, you first have to accept that living a longer life also means adopting the mindset that you will live a longer *youthful* life, not a longer life of infirmity. This is where the concept of juvenescence comes in.

The word "juvenescence" first appeared in English usage in the early 1800s, but the word is actually of ancient origin. It comes from the Latin verb *juvenesco*, which to the Romans meant "to grow young again, to become vigorous, regain strength, and flourish."[22] Stanford Professor Robert Pogue Harrison reintroduced the term to 21st-century audiences with his book of the same name: *Juvenescence*. The book highlights what he calls a "biocultural transformation that is turning large segments of the human population into 'younger' species—younger in looks, behavior, mentality, lifestyles, and above all, desires."[23] He makes the point that if we are going to live longer and look younger, we are also going to have to think and behave as we did when we were younger, not in an immature way but in a creative, mindful way. In fact, we may have no choice but to adopt this mindset. Visionary entrepreneurs Jim Mellon and Al Chalabi, authors of *Juvenescence: Investing in the Age of Longevity*, reach a conclusion many of you will find stunning. The authors declare that the majority of us will not have enough money to retire at age 65, which directly contradicts the traditional retirement most people envision.[24] For decades, conventional retirement has occurred at the end of a linear three-phase life: learn, earn, and adjourn, where "adjourning" means permanently quitting work for income by age 65. This traditional vision continues to dominate the thinking of most financial advisors and their clients.

Perhaps we hang on to the vision because it's so straightforward, therefore requiring little imagination or creativity. The goal is the same for everyone: become financially independent in your mid-60s by having accumulated enough assets and income to fund your chosen lifestyle for the rest of your life. In short, it means reaching the point where work is optional, so you can look forward to leisure time, doing activities of your own choosing for the rest of your life. But how much leisure time do you really want? Let's say you retire at age 65 but live to be 100. You would have over 12,700 days or 203,200 hours of free time! That's not only a lot of time to fill but also, and maybe more importantly, a lot of time to fund. For this reason, if you already have a retirement plan, we suggest asking your advisor to run two financial planning scenarios for you, one that takes you to age 100 and another that takes you to 105. Indeed, some of you will be wealthy enough to afford retirement at age 65 and have your income streams and assets take you that far, living the life you want to live. However, it's far more likely that your plan will reveal that you could very well run out of money long before you run out of life. Even more sobering is the thought that the life you are able to fund may not be a life you find fulfilling.

This brings us back to the essential concept of juvenescence, planning for a youthful life far beyond what we traditionally thought would be the case. With the anticipated scientific breakthroughs on the horizon, having a spirit of juvenescence calls for recapturing some of our youthfulness as we grow older. Gratton and Scott wrote, "A 100-year life with its multiple stages and several transitions requires flexibility and plasticity, so retaining adolescent features into adulthood will become more useful."[25] One of the key questions we all had to answer when we were young displays such flexibility and plasticity: "What do you want to be when you grow up?" If fact, you were being asked what you wanted to be from the time you were old enough to talk, and your answers likely changed many times as you aged. As an adult, professionally speaking, you answered this question decades ago, but the Longevity Revolution necessitates that you once again ask yourself what you "want to be" for the next three or four decades of your life. Granted, you could fritter away that vast expanse of time; people do it all the time. But wouldn't you rather approach that time in an intentional, purposeful way? Wouldn't you rather create an inspiring longevity plan that includes life-enhancing goals conceived in a spirit of juvenescence?

Robert Frost's poem "The Road Not Taken" speaks about choosing the road less traveled over the more well-traveled road, thereby forsaking the choice most people make. Consider the possibility that as an aspiring centenarian embracing juvenescence, you may have time to double-back and take both roads, forsaking nothing in the process! Increased time for living means more opportunities for "both/ands" and fewer "either/ors." Why stop at two roads? You might take both and, along the way, discover even more roads you want to explore. The vision of an active life as a centenarian calls for the spirit of exploration and creativity in retirement that originally came with the transition from childhood to adolescence to adulthood.

# The Road Less Traveled:
# A Nontraditional Retirement

At the 2019 World Economic Forum in Davos, Switzerland, the global research and consulting firm Mercer presented a workshop titled "Redesigning Later Life," which led to the suggestion that going forward, we will face "a multistage life, with periods of later-life learning, part-time work or multiple careers, and phased retirement taking center stage."[26] In other words, the Longevity Revolution means most people will travel a meandering road toward financial independence, reaching their destination much later than age 65. In fact, setting our sights on financial independence at 65 with money that lasts until age 100 or beyond would require more self-sacrifice than most of us are willing to make. The strenuous, grinding effort at saving and investing and the consequent self-denial would mean foregoing spending money on several interim goals or personal pleasures along the way. Who wants to live like that? In addition to the extra income that working past age 65 affords us, as Americans, we reap the benefit of a significantly increased Social Security payment if we wait to retire later than age 65. For all those reasons, in the age of longevity, most people will work beyond their 60s—like it or not. The key is finding a way to like it, but how do you ensure that's what happens? Taking the "road less traveled" involves exploring new questions and thinking in creative ways about answers. Here are some ways to do just that.

1. **Continue to work full time beyond age 65 in your current position**

   While this way of proceeding is not very creative, it is a viable option for those who both like their work and like the people they work with. If that's your situation, why stop at age 65? Why stop doing what you like to do? Why not work another 5 or 10 years to ensure financial independence for the 100+year life? To be sure, some professions in the U.S., such as commercial airline pilot, mandate retirement at age 65 as a safety precaution. Most people, however, work in jobs that have no mandatory retirement age, so they can continue full-time work long past age 65.

Nevertheless, financial advisors well know that even people who like their work might reach a point where doing the job full time becomes too much of a good thing. If that's your situation, consider how to mitigate what you don't like. If having more free time is an issue, negotiate more paid (or unpaid) vacation time. If the work itself is getting monotonous, request to be put on a new project. If someone on your team rubs you the wrong way, ask if you can be moved to a new team. The point is this: On the whole, if you like your job, do what you can to keep it until you achieve your financial independence for the 100+year life.

2. **Cut back from full-time to part-time work in your current occupation**

If you like your job and co-workers but don't want full-time work past a certain age, explore the option of working part time—maybe three or four days per week or fewer hours each day—in the same job. If you can work part time in your career into your 70s or 80s, you are creating a juvenescent way of preparing for the 100+year life. If your employer can't or won't accommodate your desire to go part time, you might want to consider working for a competitor, working in a related field, or starting a consulting business of your own. Working for yourself is an especially attractive option, allowing you to establish your own work schedule and take as much vacation as you want.

3. **Take a "bow" and come back for an encore career**

With this creative strategy, you take a "bow" (i.e., retire) and completely exit your current work world. However, not being finished with your performing years, you then go back to work in a new "encore" career. Granted, selecting an encore career from all the possible options may call for more juvenescent exploration and creativity than you currently possess. Fortunately, a number of resources are available to help you envision a second (or third or fourth) career. A classic in this area, one many of us first encountered during our college years, is *What Color is Your Parachute?: A Practical Manual for Job-Hunters and Career-Changers* by Richard N. Bolles. In print since the '70s and updated annually, this book has sold millions of copies, making it the most popular book on the subject of careers. Another great resource is *Mid-Life Career Rescue: The Call for Change 2020* by Cassandra Gaisford, which includes practical quizzes and activities. In addition to these written resources, there are also human resources, such as life coaches, who specialize in helping people through transitions and can assist with this visioning process.

### 4. Create a Portfolio of Activities

Creating a portfolio of activities, which Gratton and Scott call "the portfolio zone," means you don't have to make a single choice at all. Instead, the portfolio approach allows you to take on a variety of activities for income at the same time.[27] Gratton and Scott make the important point that building a portfolio is not age dependent; it can be done at any stage in life. Emilie Wapnick, the award-winning author of *How to Be Everything: A Guide for Those Who (Still) Don't Know What They Want to Be When They Grow Up*, suggests that those who enjoy many different types of work and have many different skills are not aimless or lost. On the contrary, they are "multipotentialites"—those who pursue many interests and have potential in multiple areas. She speaks of the "myth of the one true calling," freeing us to explore the other projects or pursuits that tug at us and maybe have for years.

Ultimately, whether you choose to keep working full time in your current position, cut back to part time in your current occupation, take a "bow" and come back for an encore career, or establish a portfolio of activities, the difference between nontraditional and traditional retirement is whether or not to continue to work for income into your 70s or later. Either way, the road less traveled (i.e., continued employment or other activities) and the road most traveled (i.e., traditional retirement) converge at the point of juvenescent exploration and creativity because both involve planning for a much longer, healthier, more youthful life. Such purposeful living will ultimately provide a greater incentive than any financial reward.

# A Summary of Your Longevity Planning So Far

Prior to proceeding to the exercises for your Longevity Planning Journal, let's review the longevity planning process so far. In Chapter 1, you got a sense of what is happening in aging science to create the possibility of healthy longevity to age 100 and beyond. You reflected on two questions: 1) How long do I want to live?, and 2) What passion and purpose(s) drive me?

In this chapter, we discussed the distinction between traditional retirement in a person's early to mid-60s and a nontraditional retirement that involves working for income, either by choice or by necessity, until age 70 and beyond. As long as you have enough income and assets to fund the 100+year life, either the traditional or nontraditional road will work, but both roads call for juvenescent exploration and creativity to make the most of one's future life in the Longevity Revolution. At this stage in the longevity planning process, it's most important for you to decide between the "two roads diverged in a yellow wood": a traditional or nontraditional retirement.

# Questions and Suggested Activities

*Consider downloading the Longevity Planning Journal document from our website, LongevityRevolutionPress.com.*

Answer the questions below, typing or writing your notes and reflections in your Longevity Planning Journal.

In a spirit of juvenescence, growing younger as you age, consider the following:

**1** When it comes to your future, do you prefer a traditional retirement, retiring at about age 65, or a nontraditional retirement, working for income beyond age 65. Why?

**2** If you want or need to choose a nontraditional retirement, you should make a preliminary selection of one of the four ways to do that, as outlined in this chapter. Check the appropriate box in front of one of the following four options:

❏ 1. Continue to work full time beyond age 65 in my current position.

❏ 2. Cut back from full-time to part-time work in my current occupation.

❏ 3. Take a "bow" and come back for an encore career.

❏ 4. Create a portfolio of activities.

If you chose the third option, what would you like your encore career to be and why?

If you chose the fourth option, creating a portfolio, write about the number and kinds of activities you would like to be involved in to generate income.

**3**

# Identifying Core Values for Longevity Planning

Whether pursuing a traditional retirement or a nontraditional one that includes working for income later in life, you will need to make some important decisions to effectively answer the question, **"How can I make my potential 100+year life the most fulfilling it can be?"** Having talked with hundreds of retirees, we hear one consistent, clear message: Make sure your key choices are aligned with your core values. While we can all name values we hold, the most important among them are core values. The word "core" has to do with the root of something. Core values are so deeply held that, together with your passion and purpose(s), they encompass your own personal "true north" for flourishing in the Longevity Revolution. Clearly, core values can change over time because your way of being can shift over time. For example, some values you had when you were younger may be quite different from the values you have now; you may have let go of some values and adopted others as your life progressed.

Although identifying your values for thriving later in life is essential for wise financial planning, many financial advisors bypass this important discussion and proceed directly to setting financial goals because they can more quickly and easily be attached to numbers, to amounts of money needed to reach them.

While identifying financial goals is certainly a necessary part of the planning process, that discussion should always follow a discussion about the core values that make your life rewarding.

At the beginning of the millennium, Bill Bachrach published a book that underscores this point, *Values-Based Financial Planning: The Art of Creating an Inspiring Financial Strategy*. In Bachrach's well-defined and helpful process, core values are revealed through a client-advisor conversation that begins with the question, "What's important about money to you?" The client's core values then lead to building a "values staircase" that fits well with Abraham Maslow's original hierarchy of needs (that eventually became structured as a pyramid). As the values conversation unfolds, the lower level of the values staircase (akin to the base of the pyramid) deals with safety and security concerns (e.g., having enough money to pay the bills), the mid-level values deal with key relationships and activities, and the highest-level values deal with what Maslow himself described as self-actualizing values (e.g., "being the best person I can be," or "making sure my life has purpose"). The core values identified through *Values-Based Financial Planning* can be called descriptive values, those that people already hold and that accurately describe what is important to them.

We will build on Bachrach's work in two ways. First, we will offer an alternative to a hierarchical staircase or pyramid, and second, we will discuss prescriptive values, those needed for planning and thriving in a potential 100+year life.

# From Maslow's Pyramid to Kaufman's Sailboat

Dr. Scott Barry Kaufman, Scientific Director of the Imagination Institute at the University of Pennsylvania, in his book *Transcend: The New Science of Self-Actualization*, reimagined Maslow's pyramid and offered a new image—a sailboat—thereby significantly advancing Maslow's work. Kaufman makes the point that life is not a trek up a summit where, once you arrive, you just stay, having fulfilled all your needs and desires once and for all. Human life just doesn't work that way.

Instead, Kaufman envisions life more like a vast ocean of choices and experiences. This ocean is full of new opportunities for meaning and purpose, but it is also a journey in which we encounter stormy weather, with times of danger and uncertainty. As a result, a recurring need for safety and security can appear throughout the course of one's life. When one's need for safety and security is threatened, it's time to pause more enjoyable activities in order to "batten down the hatches." In good times, with safety and security needs well taken care of, one can set sail for personal growth opportunities that lead to new experiences and a more fulfilling life.

Connecting Kaufman's sailboat image to core values, the hull of the sailboat might represent safety and security values, while the sail might represent growth values. The safety and security core values are those that allow for personal strength during the "stormy seas" of life. The growth core values are those that allow you to sail to new "ports of call" (i.e., new life experiences) in the future, as well as revisit familiar "ports of call" (i.e., favorite life experiences) again and again.

We believe the sailboat image is much stronger than a staircase or pyramid because the image of sailing on an ocean of choices and experiences better captures the vast possibilities and experiences in the over 12,700 days beyond age 65 of your potential 100+year life. It also allows for the interplay of safety and security issues along with growth opportunities. Again, when stormy seas make an appearance in your life, your goals for flourishing may need to be postponed or altered to give sufficient energy and attention to your safety and security. On the other hand, when it's smooth sailing, you might accomplish some goals faster than you thought, or you might add new goals.

You'll want your "sailboat" headed in the direction of healthy transcendence or self-actualization in terms of peak experiences that involve, as Kaufman puts it, "heightened joy, serenity, beauty, and wonder." Creating an excellent longevity plan based on your core values allows you to thrive in the Longevity Revolution.

# Prescriptive Core Values for Longevity

If you haven't yet fully internalized the possibilities of the Longevity Revolution described earlier in this book, your planning might be hit or miss when it comes to identifying and owning the core values needed to make the most of a much longer, healthier life. In truth, certain values are so important, so foundational, for the Longevity Revolution that if you don't currently have these values among your personal core list, you will need to adopt them. For that reason, we label these prescriptive core values, those you must have to join the Longevity Revolution. In effect, we have been encouraging you to adopt some of these prescriptive core values as you have been reading this book.

From the first chapter, you have been encouraged to embrace **healthy longevity** with the aim of living the 100+year life. (More on the subject of health is found in the next chapter.) Although millions embrace living a healthy lifestyle while they are young, the vast majority of people, unfortunately, do not have healthy longevity as a core value because their image of old age is not positive. They don't yet perceive that they could personally benefit from the coming scientific advances that will help deliver the 100+year healthy life.

Up to this point in your life, you might have even taken your health for granted. If so, it's time to change that. If you would not have previously listed "healthy longevity" among your core values, you need to do so now. By definition, you can't join the Longevity Revolution without your health, and although science can do a lot, science can't do it all for you.

In addition to healthy longevity, this book has encouraged you to embrace the importance of **long-life learning**, **passion** for your purpose(s), and **creativity** and **exploration**. However, there are two more core values we have not yet mentioned that qualify as necessary or prescriptive for flourishing longevity.

First, your list must include the value of personal **happiness**. In fact, happiness is so important for human flourishing that it has been written about since the time of the earliest Greek philosophers, including Aristotle (384–322 B.C.E), who considered happiness the goal of human thought and action. Fast forwarding in time, in recent decades happiness has become the subject of scientific study. Martin Seligman, professor of psychology and one of the most prominent researchers on happiness, wrote *Flourish: A Visionary New Understanding of Happiness and Well Being,* that uses interactive exercises aimed at growing personal happiness.

Whereas happiness is so important that we consider it a universal core value for longevity planning, the "pursuit of happiness" can be easily misunderstood as nothing more than pleasure-seeking behavior or having a constant state of intense positive emotions. To be sure, happiness has an emotional impact, but it doesn't have to be understood in terms of a constant feeling of joy. Dr. Ed Diener and his son Dr. Robert Biswas-Diener provide helpful clarification on happiness:

> We recommend that people think of happiness in terms of mildly pleasant emotions that are felt most of the time, with the intense positive emotions being felt occasionally. If you feel fairly energetic and upbeat most of the time on most days, and are generally satisfied with your life with only the occasional complaint, you are, by our definition, happy. Some of us will feel more intense emotions and some of us less intense emotions due to our different temperaments, but frequent positive emotions should be the goal, rather than continuing intense feelings.[28]

Another researcher doing innovative work on happiness is Dan Buettner, who joins happiness and longevity in a powerful way. Buettner's research on longevity goes back over 20 years and led to his creating Blue Zones, a company that helps people live longer, happier lives. As Buettner explains, Blue Zones are areas in the world that have a relatively high percentage of healthy centenarians. In 2017, he published *The Blue Zones of Happiness: Lessons from the World's Happiest People*, which includes specific strategies involving community, work, home, and self. Together, the strategies result in happiness-boosting habits. As the late motivational speaker Jim Rohn once said, "Happiness is not by accident." On the contrary, happiness is on purpose. Because happiness is on purpose, we want you to know that you can plan for it. That is why we want you to make happiness a core life value and integrate your personal pursuit of happiness into your longevity plan.

The last fundamental core value for longevity planning is having a **growth mindset** (or attitude). Of all the core values, this is the one meta-value that encompasses all the other prescriptive longevity core values: growth in healthy longevity, growth in long-life learning, growth in the ability to explore, growth in creativity and exploration, growth in purpose(s) and passion, and growth in happiness. Having a growth mindset means that rather than these areas being stuck or set, you truly believe you can enhance, add to, or change them by having a positive "can do" attitude about your ability to do so. A growth mindset puts you in control of making your 100+year life the most fulfilling it can be.

The innovative Modern Elder Academy showcases the importance of having a growth mindset later in life using the work of Dr. Carol Dweck, professor of psychology at Stanford University. Her work illustrates the power of our most basic beliefs, those that make up our "mindset." Whether conscious or subconscious, these beliefs affect both what we want and whether we succeed in getting it. In short, our mindset either propels us toward or prevents us from achieving our potential as it relates to longevity planning.

Applying Dweck's work to values, if you believe that your core values are unchangeable at this stage of your life or that you cannot add to or grow new core values moving forward, then you have a fixed mindset vis-à-vis your values. That fixed mindset will be a self-fulfilling prophecy: you *won't* grow because you think you *can't* grow. Therefore, if you think your core values are set in stone at this stage of your life, guess what? You're right. For *you*, they *are* fixed. But if you adopt a growth mindset and believe core values are flexible and changeable, you're right, too! For you, they are flexible and changeable! In the spirit of juvenescence described earlier, you can adapt your life to the values needed for joining the Longevity Revolution.

Keep in mind that the prescriptive core values for the Longevity Revolution (listed below for reference) are all growth values, the "sail" of your sailboat.

- Healthy longevity
- Long-life learning
- Creativity and Exploration
- Passion for your purpose(s)
- Happiness
- Growth Mindset

In the exercises at the end of the chapter, we'll add one prescriptive core value that relates to safety and security, the "hull" of your boat: **sufficient financial resources for the 100+year life**. You will work on this core value with your financial advisor to help identify sufficient financial resources to help meet your goals for your potential 100+year life.

# Descriptive Core Values

Of course, the prescriptive core values for longevity are not the only important core values you hold. We focused on prescriptive core values first because they are essential in the Longevity

Revolution. As we mentioned earlier, there are also important descriptive core values, values that you have internalized and may have been functioning in your life for decades. These are the values that have given your life direction down to the present day. They are values you may have internalized from your childhood experiences, your family, your education, your place of worship, your work, your friends, and your life experiences. They include values such as marriage, family, friendship, faith, integrity, compassion, etc. You likely already know what these descriptive core values are and how they function in your life, even if you haven't ever formally named or listed them.

In the core values exercise that follows, you will be asked to identify values for the Longevity Revolution in two categories: (1) safety and security, and (2) growth. In some cases, a core value can show up in both categories. For example, for many people, religious faith is vital for weathering the storms of life, so it is a core safety and security value; however, religious faith may be a growth value as well (i.e., a desire to grow in your faith). As such, religious faith would appear in both categories on the chart. Taken together, all your prescriptive and descriptive values will be used to help you set inspiring goals as you complete your Personal Longevity Plan (Chapter 9).

# Questions and Suggested Activities

*Consider downloading the Longevity Planning Journal document from our website, LongevityRevolutionPress.com.*

**1** This exercise helps you identify core values for longevity planning and claim them as your own. The top quadrants of the chart on the next page, quadrants 1 and 2, represent core values related to growth (your "sail"), while the bottom quadrants, 3 and 4, represent values related to safety and security (your "hull").

In quadrants 1 and 3, you will find that we have already listed the prescriptive values necessary for the Longevity Revolution. Whether or not you would have embraced these values before you read this book, we hope you understand that they are vital for joining the Longevity Revolution and planning for the 100+year life.

Quadrants 2 and 4 are where you have the opportunity to record your personal values related to growth as well as safety and security. Note that there is no set number of descriptive core values you should have. However many core values you believe describe your life are the right number for you.

# Longevity Core Values

| | QUADRANT 1 | QUADRANT 2 |
|---|---|---|
| **CORE GROWTH VALUES** | **Prescriptive Core Growth Values for the Longevity Revolution**<br><br>• Long-life Learning<br><br>• Creativity & Exploration<br><br>• Passion<br><br>• Happiness<br><br>• Growth Mindset<br><br>• Healthy Longevity | **Descriptive Core Growth Values for the Longevity Revolution (identified by you)**<br><br>• _____<br><br>• _____<br><br>• _____<br><br>• _____<br><br>• _____ |
| | **QUADRANT 3** | **QUADRANT 4** |
| **CORE SAFETY & SECURITY VALUES** | **Prescriptive Core Safety & Security Values for the Longevity Revolution**<br><br>• Healthy Longevity<br><br>• Sufficient Financial Resources for the 100+year Life | **Descriptive Core Safety & Security Values for the Longevity Revolution (identified by you)**<br><br>• _____<br><br>• _____<br><br>• _____<br><br>• _____<br><br>• _____ |

**2** In your journal, beginning with Quadrant 1 and moving through the other three, write a few sentences or phrases about each core value by reflecting on this question: How can I enhance this value as an important part of my life in the coming decades?

**3** How do your reflections make you feel? Are you excited and inspired to participate in the Longevity Revolution?

# 4

# Adopting and Enhancing Habits for Healthy Longevity

As mentioned in the previous chapter, having healthy longevity on your list of core values is essential for joining the Longevity Revolution. Whatever your current health habits are, this chapter will encourage you to take them to the next level. A growth mindset regarding your health means fostering the positive "can do" attitude that you have the potential and ability to get healthier in the future than you are now. Even if you consider your present health very good, there is likely room for intentional improvement. Moreover, improving your health habits can make a huge positive difference, both in your ability to live longer and the degree to which you will enjoy that longer life.

## A Mindset for Healthy Longevity

At this point in your life, you may have tried many ways to be healthier, dabbling in diets or exercise routines that never quite became "routine." You may have lost weight only to gain it back, lost it again, and gained it back—again and again. Almost everyone has had this experience. New Year's resolutions often focus on health, but too often, the "new" becomes "old" before

February 1. Perhaps the failure of such resolutions is as simple as not having a sufficient reason to pursue better health. "Looking better" in the eyes of others or feeling better in clothes that have become too tight are likely not strong enough motivations. We believe that embracing a vision for a healthy 100+year life is the missing ingredient, the deeper, more powerful reason for adopting and maintaining habits for longevity. What if you started believing that you could gift yourself an extra two or three decades of health and vitality? Might that be the incentive you need to provide sustained interest, motivation, and, ultimately, success at enhancing your health habits? The very desire to join the Longevity Revolution can deliver the growth mindset that says, "Yes! Healthy longevity is one of my core values. Yes! I'm going to do what it takes to advance my health habits. Yes, I *can* do it! Yes, I *will* do it!"

At the same time, a growth mindset for healthy longevity aims for progress, not perfection. A growth mindset stays open to the possibility of altering behaviors less conducive to health and establishing or enhancing habits more conducive to health. Realizing that there is often a psychosomatic (i.e., mind-body) connection to good health, we present health habits in two broad categories: 1) habits to enhance physical health, and 2) habits to enhance brain health.

However, we must cover a couple of important caveats before we begin. First, we are neither medical professionals nor health experts. What we offer here is gleaned from the research and wisdom of others, which is referenced in the text and/or in endnotes. We try to make the suggestions general enough to apply to most people, but this leads to the second caveat. You should consult your physician prior to making any changes to your health habits. Your personal physician may have good reason to suggest other ways to promote your goal of healthy longevity. So please accept the ideas we provide in the spirit in which they are intended, as general suggestions for adopting and enhancing habits for healthy longevity that are to be discussed with your personal physician prior to implementation.

# Enhancing Habits for Physical Health
## Eating Well

The number of books, articles, and research reports on healthy diets seems to be endless, and much of what is written—even by medical experts—offers conflicting advice. Various diets have their "day in the sun" and quickly fade away as the fads they were, so we are cautious about suggesting anything definitive other than the most basic, widely accepted ideas:

- Add fiber to your meals by eating more fruits, vegetables, and whole grains.

- Consider eating more organic food. It sometimes costs a bit more but helps avoid potentially damaging chemicals. (As with questions about health information, the jury is still out on what truly is healthfully produced food. Our belief is to eat food that has had as little human manipulation as possible.)

- Eat balanced meals and avoid saturated fats.

- Eat less sodium (salt).

- Eat less sugar.

- Drink alcohol in moderation.

Beyond the basics, it is important to be aware of work done by longevity experts who have written about diets from the standpoint of promoting healthy longevity.

Dan Buettner, introduced in the previous chapter, promotes the Blue Zones Diet, which emphasizes eating until one is 80 percent full and no more. He offers the following practical guidelines, some of which echo our general suggestions:

1. Eat a mostly plant-based diet.

2. Cut down on meat. People in four of the five Blue Zones consume meat, but they do so sparingly, using it as a celebratory food, a small side, or a way to flavor dishes. Five times a month would be ideal.

3. Eat fish, fewer than three ounces, up to three times weekly.

4. Reduce dairy products.

5. Eat eggs. People in all the Blue Zones eat eggs two to four times per week.

6. Eat at least a half cup of cooked beans daily.

7. Cut back on sugar. Consume no more than seven teaspoons (28 grams) of added sugar daily.

8. Snack on nuts, two handfuls per day.

9. Limit bread to sourdough or 100 percent whole wheat.

10. Eat natural rather than processed foods.

11. Drink mainly water. Avoid soft drinks. With few exceptions, people in Blue Zones drink primarily coffee, tea, water, and wine.[29]

For those interested in more information, Buettner has published *The Blue Zones Kitchen*, a cookbook with 100 recipes inspired by Blue Zones locations around the world.

Beyond eating well, the other way to enhance physical health is by becoming more fit. Much like diets, there are too many physical fitness ideas and programs—again, many of which conflict—to review in this brief book, so we will simply highlight some basic exercise habits that the research associates with longevity.

## Stretching

Miranda Esmonde-White's *New York Times* bestseller *Aging Backwards* provides helpful information about how small, consistent movements that engage all of the body's muscles and connective tissues keep us strong, flexible, and young. In addition, she provides new insights into aging science. In particular, she explains the necessity of engaging the fascia— the collagen-rich connective tissue that protects, supports, and literally binds our body together—to prevent joint problems, arthritis, stiffness, and injury.[30]

Many people also enjoy the ancient practice of yoga, a more intense form of stretching. Classes, books, and routines are abundantly available. The point is that to stay healthy longer, a body needs to be flexible enough to move with ease!

## Walking

Fitness books and exercise gurus agree on the benefits of simply walking. Whether you walk outdoors or on a treadmill, you will benefit from doing so. Walking helps the cardiovascular system, aids digestion, releases good endorphins, and allows you to enjoy every season of nature's wonders. A long walk can also single-handedly result in a positive attitude adjustment. When you walk outside with your head held high and your eyes forward, you get a break from whatever might be bringing you down.

How much to walk remains a question. According to the Mayo Clinic, the average American walks about 3,000 to 4,000 steps per day or 1.5 to 2.0 miles. With the advent of fitness trackers, the goal became 10,000 steps a day, about five miles. However, if you are trying to lose weight, you may want to aim for a higher goal.[31]

## Cardiovascular Exercising

"Cardio" exercises include brisk walking, biking, running, swimming, and a host of other exercises that can be done on exercise equipment. The focus here, of course, is any activity that makes your heart beat faster, thereby strengthening the heart and lungs. Like any other muscle, the heart and lungs become stronger with regular physical activity. As your cardiovascular fitness improves, your heart muscle won't have to work as forcefully to pump oxygen-rich blood through your body. Most experts agree that healthy adults should get at least 150 minutes, or 30 minutes five times a week, of moderate cardiovascular exercise.[32]

## Strength Training

Particularly important after age 60, strength or resistance training builds both muscle strength and endurance. In addition, strength training helps maintain bone density. Strength training is usually done with free weights, strength-training machines, or resistance bands, but you can also use your own body (e.g., by doing push-ups). The American College of Sports Medicine provides these guidelines, but again, check with your physician:

- Perform 8 to 10 exercises that stress the major muscle groups.

- Perform 2 to 3 sets of 8 to 12 repetitions, with the last repetition being difficult to complete.

- Lift and lower the weight in a controlled manner (2 seconds up and 2 seconds down).

- Perform strength exercises 2 to 3 times per week.

- Increase the amount of weight lifted over time so that the difficulty level feels like an 8 out of 10 (where 0=no effort, 10= hardest effort you can give).[33]

## Getting a More Restful Night's Sleep

Getting a good night's sleep is key to healthy aging, with most professionals agreeing that adults need 7 to 8 hours of sleep each night. According to a study published by the *European Heart Journal*, the best time to fall asleep is between 10 p.m. and 11 p.m. People who fell asleep during this window of time were found to have a lower risk of heart disease than those who fell asleep earlier or later.[34]

Johns Hopkins sleep expert Rachel Salas shares the following suggestions for daily life to help ensure that you get enough rest:

**Morning suggestions:**
- Eat breakfast by a window or outdoors so the sun can help reset your circadian clock.

- Make your bed. People who do so are more likely to sleep better at night.
- Wake up at the same time every morning, including weekends and holidays.

**Afternoon suggestions:**

- Exercise at lunch. Early workouts may sacrifice sleep, and those within 3 hours of bed may keep you awake.
- Cut caffeine by 4 p.m.—or noon if you are sensitive. Its effects can linger for 4 more hours.
- If you take a nap, take it before 3 p.m., and keep it to 30 minutes or less.

**Evening suggestions:**

- Use lamps and dimmers. Bright overhead lights trick your brain into thinking it's still daytime.
- Keep showers or baths warm (not hot). Also, turn down the thermostat a few degrees to mimic your nighttime drop in body temperature.
- Turn off technology 30 minutes before bed. Blue light and constant stimulation make it tough to wind down.
- Have a light before-bed snack—yogurt or fruit—if hunger often wakes you.
- Stick to the same bedtime, or vary it by no more than an hour.[35]

## Achieving Normal, Healthy Medical Numbers

In 2021, Michael Roizen, Chief Wellness Officer Emeritus of the Cleveland Clinic, gave a presentation at the Global Wellness Summit, where he shared what he called the "6 Normals + 2" for a healthy life. Specifically, the six "normals" refer to numerical readings in six important health-related categories. The additional two refer to (1) seeing a primary care physician every year, and (2) keeping your immunizations up to date. The medical readings Dr. Roizen recommends for the "6 normals" are:

1. Blood pressure that is less than 125/85 (systolic/diastolic).

2. A Body Mass Index (BMI) of 21 to 29.9, or a waist that measures less than half your height.

3. A fasting blood sugar of less than 107.

4. LDL (bad) cholesterol less than 100.

5. Zero Cotinine [evidence of tobacco use] in urine.

6. One completed stress management course.[36]

## Fostering a Sense of Humor and Laughter

In the 1960s, Norman Cousins, editor of the prestigious literary journal *Saturday Review*, discovered the importance of humor to health when he was diagnosed with an incurable disease of the connective tissue that caused constant, excruciating pain every moment of his life. The prognosis was that the pain would only get worse, leading to an early death, but he remembered reading a medical study that said negative emotions directly affect the adrenal glands. He surmised if this were true, perhaps positive emotions brought on by humor would work to positively affect his body. Pursuing this, Cousins found that watching funny television shows and films that made him laugh allowed him to sleep pain free for two hours. In a matter of months, the "incurable disease" completely disappeared. As a result, Cousins quit his job at the *Saturday Review*, repurposed his life, and joined the faculty at UCLA's medical school where he formed a humor and medicine task force.[37]

While we aren't saying that laughter is a cure-all for disease, according to the Mayo Clinic, laughter can induce positive physical changes in the body by stimulating many organs, relieving stress, decreasing blood pressure, stimulating circulation and muscle relaxation, improving the immune system, and relieving pain. Of course, there are attitudinal benefits as well, including improving personal satisfaction and lessening anxiety.[38] In fact, laughter is considered so powerful that the Mbuti hunter-gathers of northeast Zaire use it to dissipate intertribal quarrels. Better yet, laughter comes at no cost to any of us. It is a natural gift we can all access, so seek good humor often. The benefits are bound to be positive.

## Enhancing Brain Health

In addition to enhancing physical health habits, enhancing your brain health is needed for healthy longevity. In the 1990s, long before the idea of the Longevity Revolution was conceived, the CBS news magazine *48 Hours* aired an hour-long special on aging and health. A segment on brain research showed the frontal lobe scans from the brains of a 21-year-old and an 80-year-old. The differences were clear. The 21-year-old's scan had many areas appearing in red, which represented signs of an active mind. Indeed, this young person was attending college and generally felt optimistic about life. In contrast, the 80-year-old's scan was completely gray, showing no color at all. Despite having no major illnesses, this older person was sedentary, alone, and uninvolved in life. The exciting news came when the researcher said that brain scans of many other older people looked identical to those of the younger person! These older people—we could call them longevity pioneers—were still actively using their brains and their bodies, and their brain scans showed that. "We believe in the 'use it or lose it' approach to mental health and aging," the researcher said.

Today, doctors and scientists continue this research on brain health. One of the most interesting books dealing with this topic in relation to longevity, *Successful Aging: A Neuroscientist Explores the Power and Potential of Our Lives*, was written by Daniel J. Levitin. The author makes the interesting point that the positive personality trait of conscientiousness is important to brain health, but what does it mean to be conscientious? Levitin says it means being practical, careful, responsible, and organized. If this doesn't describe you today, with a growth mindset, you know you can become more conscientious in the future.

Beyond conscientiousness, Levitin makes the point that exercise, such as that discussed earlier, promotes brain health as well as physical health. Furthermore, he suggests that when engaging in physical exercise, it's good to get out of the gym and exercise in natural situations, such as hiking on trails, because doing so stimulates the brain along with the body. Likewise, brain health requires social interaction, so why not exercise with others? A study from the Karolinska Institute showed that people with strong social networks were 60 percent less likely to develop dementia.[39]

Levitin also notes that meditation helps the brain become more effective and efficient as well as provides an anti-inflammatory effect. Science has demonstrated positive structural changes in the learning and memory part of the brain for those who meditated daily over many years. Levitin writes, "Even brief meditation reduces fatigue and anxiety and increases visuo-spatial processing, working memory, and executive functioning, and in many cases these benefits persist even after the meditation practice has stopped."[40] If you are new to meditation, many video guides are available online, two of which we reference in this chapter's Questions and Suggested Activities.

These benefits notwithstanding, the most exciting discovery about the brain is its "plasticity," its ability for rejuvenation. According to neuroscientists, our brain can change at any age! When we learn new things, new neural pathways are created. However, the opposite is also true. If we are not using our current pathways, they become weaker and less functional. So, whether you are age 9 or 90, your brain has the capability to change for the better or for the worse. This plasticity with respect to brain health supports the emphasis we have placed on having a growth mindset as a core value for longevity.

Levitin ends his book by sharing 10 specific ideas for rejuvenating your brain that serve as an excellent overall summary of healthy habits for flourishing longevity:

1. Don't retire. Don't stop being engaged with meaningful [paid or unpaid] work.

2. Look forward. Don't look back. (Reminiscing doesn't promote health.)

3. Exercise. Get your heart rate going, preferably in nature.

4. Embrace a moderate lifestyle with healthy practices.

5. Keep your social circle exciting and new.

6. Spend time with people younger than you.

7. See your doctor regularly, but not obsessively.

8. Don't think of yourself as old (other than taking prudent precautions).

9. Appreciate your cognitive strengths—pattern recognition, crystallized intelligence, wisdom, and accumulated knowledge.

10. Promote cognitive health through experiential learning: traveling, spending time with grandchildren, and immersing yourself in new activities. Do new things.[41]

# Questions and Suggested Activities

*Consider downloading the Longevity Planning Journal document from our website, LongevityRevolutionPress.com.*

Use your journal to record answers to the following questions.

**1** How would you rate your overall current health? To what extent do you believe you can improve it?

**2** After reflecting on the section titled "Eating Well," what items do you want to subtract or add to your diet? What other changes do you want to make?

**3** Explain the degree to which physical fitness is part of your personal wellness plan. Is your current physical fitness plan easy to follow on a weekly basis? If not, what part of it is difficult? Does your physical fitness plan include stretching? Cardiovascular exercise (including brisk walks)? Strength training?

**4** Make a list of things you are currently doing to promote a good night's sleep. Make another list of suggestions you found in this chapter that you can implement to help you sleep better.

**5** If you have them available, write down your numbers for:

- Blood pressure

- Body Mass Index or waist size

- Fasting blood sugar

- LDL cholesterol

- Cotinine (i.e., Do you use tobacco?)

If you don't know these numbers, be sure to get them at your next check-up.

**6** Have you taken a stress-reduction workshop or watched online videos on stress management? If not, when and how might you do that?

**7** What makes you laugh? How could you add more humor to your life?

8 Would you describe yourself as a "conscientious person"? Would those closest to you describe you this way? If not, what would you need to change to become more conscientious?

9 When was the last time you took a walk or hike in the woods? How can you increase the time you spend in nature?

10 Describe your week in terms of social interaction with others. Is there anything you would like to do more often or less often to enhance your opportunities for social interaction?

**11**  Do you have a daily practice of meditation or other ways to clear and calm your mind? If not, go to YouTube.com and search for "one-minute meditation."[42] After trying it, journal about this brief experience.

If you want a longer yet manageable video, try this excellent 15-minute guided meditation based on the work of Jon Kabat-Zinn, led by Vicki Panagotacos, Ph.D. On YouTube.com, search for "Mindfulness Meditation—Quick 15 Min Stress Relief Version."[43] It will likely take more than one attempt to get comfortable with and benefit from the practice of meditation, but it's worth it!

**12**  How many of Levitin's 10 items for brain health do you currently practice? If some are missing, which items would you like to add to your life?

# 5

# Building Intergenerational Relationships

How many older people do you know who talk more about their past than their present or future? And even though we know from other chapters in this book that a person's attitude toward their own aging directly and significantly affects their actual life span, how many post-retirement folks seem excited, engaged, fulfilled, and looking forward to tomorrow?

Of course, there are many reasons why older people feel as they do. Our physical aging eventually comes with costs to our bodies, despite our best efforts to eat well, get enough sleep, and properly exercise. Sometimes our willingness to work and contribute important insights based on our extensive experience can be thwarted by ageism and outright age discrimination. (There is a popular refrigerator magnet that says, "If you don't think age discrimination affects you, just wait awhile!") Many of us are concerned about Alzheimer's disease and other forms of dementia. If that happened, who would care for us, and what kind of burden would we place on those closest to us? And how many older people have their immediate families strung across the country when they simply yearn for a hug from their own children and grandchildren? These are the kinds of issues and concerns that older people have that can negatively impact their attitudes, emotions, and longevity.

Building intergenerational relationships can help these people focus on the present and look forward to the future. As we mentioned in Chapter 1, Conley and Rauth contend this kind of thinking also enhances long-life learning. Therefore, we encourage you to *intentionally* start thinking intergenerationally if you want to fully join the Longevity Revolution. The good news is that building intergenerational relationships comes with little or no financial costs. Taking some small personal risks, however, can reap rewards beyond calculation.

Start by taking a good look around you. We now have six distinct generations living in our cities, suburbs, small towns, and farming communities. Members of some or all of these different generations go to your church, synagogue, or mosque. You'll see them in shopping malls, at sporting events, concerts, plays, on cruises, vacations, golf courses—almost anywhere you go. But if you're not looking for them, they might as well not exist.

This chapter will briefly introduce you to each one of the six living generations, demonstrate the real benefits of finding and building intergenerational relationships within and outside your family, and provide some simple steps for how to connect with other generations. We can all benefit from better understanding each generation in order to relate to others beyond our own generation.

In terms of the generational values discussed, it is important to note that psychologists say we start forming our basic core values somewhere between the ages of 10 and 20, and many say that such development comes at even younger ages. As we mentioned earlier, some values stay with us while others may change as we progress through life.

It is easy to understand the influence of generational values when we look at our own families. While you may share some core values with your father, mother, children, and grandchildren, you may also hold some different values because you are a member of a different generation. These differences are largely based on the economic, educational, political, religious, cultural, and other important influences that shaped who you became when you were developing your initial value system. As we begin understanding generational differences in terms of values, we are in a better position to identify and understand our values in comparison to the values of the other five generations.

# The GI or Civic Generation (Born 1900–1931)

Around two million people are among the longevity pioneers that the former television journalist Tom Brokaw calls the "Greatest Generation." This generation came out of an agricultural economy and, as children or young adolescents, lived through the Great Depression. They were heroes in their generational hour of crisis, World War II.

After the war, this generation built the national and international corporate structure and the interstate highway system as well as enabled millions of their peers to go to college for free (through the GI Bill) and own homes (through the Federal Housing Authority). Their values included no-nonsense frugality, respect for a chain of command, loyalty, lifetime security, equality of opportunity, an international outlook, and a firm belief in the importance of family.

# The Adaptive or Mediating Generation (1932–1944)

Most of this generation, also known as the Silent Generation, came of age too late to participate in World War II and too early to participate in Vietnam, but some did serve in the Korean conflict. Experts have called them the "unobtrusive children of depression and war," "The Lonely Crowd," and "conformists." They quietly expanded the strong CEO model of the hero GIs into more complex management structures. They created and developed the human resource system and the notion of a career ladder based on merit. Dress and appearance were important to them. They were often called upon as mediators, hence the name, the Mediating Generation. Much of the social and volunteering infrastructure we still see active today, such as the Elks, Lions, Rotary, League of Women Voters, and church social justice committees, were created by this generation.

# The Boomers (1945–1963)

Boomers are the largest of the living generations, if you count immigrants, in American history. They entered college and the workplace in large numbers from the Kennedy through the Reagan administrations. This was the first generation in American history to be largely raised in a culture of abundance and to be influenced by media, especially television. Although raised in what evolved into an affluent generation, 75 percent of Boomers came from poor, working-class families whose parents, primarily farmers and small entrepreneurs, did not attend college. As a result, Boomers demonstrated both a spirit of optimism as well as hubris.

As adolescents, they watched the struggle for civil rights and sexual equality on TV. Then many of the men, still in their teen years, were drafted to fight a bloody war in Vietnam. Many became distrustful of the American ideals they heard at home, in school, and at church. They questioned authority. In the workplace, they demanded meaning, inclusiveness, and equality. They seriously questioned the lifetime security model their parents valued, but as time has shown, security has a very powerful draw.

# The Diversity Generation/
# Gen X (1964–1981)

This generation came of age in a society with increasing divorce rates, experimental educational practices, latchkey programs, an AIDS epidemic, easier access to weapons, and the highest suicide rates of any previous generation. They also have more personal multicultural experience and more proficiency with technology than the three generations that came before them.

In the workplace, they dislike process in decision making; they like being independent, self-starting, and entrepreneurial. The Diversity generation is skeptical of corporate slogans and does not value loyalty to one job or company. They see themselves as free agents who appreciate their personal time more than their work time. This is illustrated by a story about a Boomer manager talking with a Diversity employee. The manager says, "I just don't understand your generation, your work ethic, and culture." The younger worker answered, "When you were growing up, you were told that if you worked hard, you could have all the things you never had. If I work hard, it is possible I may never have all the things I have always had!"

# The Millennial Generation
# (1982–2001)

This generation developed its values in an age of test-tube babies, cloning, expansive internet apps, volatile economic times, increased educational testing, large-scale political and corporate scandals, and the most sophisticated media ever produced. Millennials all over the planet connect through the internet, lead environmental and global climate protection campaigns, fight to stop child labor, and work to beautify blighted urban neighborhoods.

Polls suggest this generation is less interested in political parties than trying to work together across generations to solve problems. They are the soldiers produced by the tragedy of 9/11, and the war on terrorism has been a major marker for their generation. They like to work in teams because most were team taught in schools. Many are still not comfortable taking risks because of their extensive experience with testing and the fear of failure.

# The Digital Generation (2002–2022)

It is still too early to tell what core values will emerge from the newest generation, the Digital Generation, but for a glimpse of what may be coming, we can look back to the time when the first Digitals came into adolescence to see what events have shaped their lives so far:

- They used technology at a very early age.
- They use interactive media more than they watch television.
- Like Millennials, they also fear failure because of the testing they experienced in school, yet they attend college at rates comparable to the Boomers.
- They like organized activities.

Only time will tell where these pivotal events will lead the Digital Generation and what generational values they will ultimately hold.

As with all quick descriptions, some things will be missing from these six generational snapshots. Still, you might want to think about your own generation or those of your extended family to see how well the descriptions fit. If you think something is missing, feel free to plug it in. The question is this: How does this generational information help equip you to become more involved in the Longevity Revolution?

# The Benefits of Intentional Intergenerational Relationships

We believe that making intentional and meaningful intergenerational connections is not only important to aging productively but also a vital aspect of longevity. Why? What are the benefits of looking at the world through both a generational and an intergenerational lens?

First, two or more generations typically mutually prosper when sharing experiences together. When you reach out to those younger or older than yourself, you will often have your spirits lifted and your optimism raised. If you don't think that's true, ask any grandparent to describe the first moment they held a new grandchild. Or watch what happens when an elderly person volunteers at a grade school. Or ask anyone in assisted living or nursing home care how they feel after receiving an unexpected visit from someone younger. Their spirits can't help but be uplifted.

Second, living intentionally intergenerationally provides the opportunity to develop new, genuine friendships and, in many circumstances, allows you to put your wisdom and experience to work with younger people seeking help in navigating an increasingly complex world. As an older person, you have the possibility of adding new chapters to your legacy by sending messages into the future through younger friends or family members. You also have the blessing of seeing the world through the eyes of someone who soon could be leading it. In short, relating across the generations can provide an increased sense of relevance to your life.

Third, we know that social isolation and loneliness can cause mental decline and earlier mortality in older men and women. Regular interaction with different generations can combat these issues and even decrease recovery time from surgeries. Meaningful relationships across the generations can also keep the mind more active and alert, one of the major steps recommended for preventing Alzheimer's and dementia. In a very real way, you can help reduce medical costs due to aging if you just begin to lead a more intentional intergenerational life.

Finally, there is the opportunity to learn new skills from another generation, either younger or older. For example, you may learn something about new technology from a younger person, or you could learn how to keep family stories and history alive from an older adult. There are plenty of skills embodied by all the living generations in your neighborhood, religious community, schools, colleges, universities, and yes, even in assisted living and nursing home facilities—if you are willing to search them out.

There is a growing awareness of the numerous benefits that come to all generations when they authentically interact. As a species, we need deep connections to all living generations to thrive. Research shows that people with close intergenerational relationships report less depression, better physical health, and higher degrees of life satisfaction. They are happier with their present and more hopeful about the future.

And this brings us to the most important part of this chapter: How we begin to make more connections across the generations, or as Maggie Kuhn, founder of the Grey Panthers, would say, "Let's inter-generate, not age segregate!" We need each other, and our society needs to appreciate and respect people of all ages, so here are some simple steps you can take to become an intentional intergenerational thinker and actor.

# Building Intergenerational Relationships Within Your Extended Family

Start with your own extended family. Make a commitment for two weeks to do the following exercise. On Sunday night, make a list of five people in your family who represent as many generations as possible other than your own. During the week, contact each person and have a conversation with them about their lives. What are they following in the media? What do they see as important issues they are dealing with? What is the last book they read or listened to? Do they feel they have enough support in their own personal networks? Add your own questions. It will be easy once the conversation begins.

If you do this for two weeks, we can almost promise you will be doing it for a long time. When you feel comfortable taking a bigger risk, try doing the same thing with people outside of your family circle.

# Building Intergenerational Relationships through Existing Programs

Many excellent intergenerational programs are available to help you get your feet wet in the intergenerational pool. These programs are often structured, which can be helpful for people who don't know where to begin. Don't make the excuse that you really can't relate to a younger or older person outside of your family because you don't understand them. You are never too old to take a personal risk, especially if that risk could be mutually beneficial.

For example, you can start with your own religious community. This is one of the last places in our society where all or most of the generations gather for reasons other than self-interest. If you have a skill, such as having parented or having run a business, or if you just want to contribute, let your pastor, rabbi, or imam know. They would be happy to connect you with someone who might need someone exactly like you.

Many other intergenerational programs are run by your local school district. These programs include mentoring students in reading or math, helping with study skills, or participating in some form of academic or athletic coaching. Sometimes just being willing to come to a school and tell your story can be helpful for young people who are eager to hear what you have to say.

You could call an assisted living facility or nursing home nearby and ask the activities director if there are people who haven't received a visitor in a long time. You might be surprised by the interesting stories such people have to tell. And remember, by visiting an older generation, you are paying it forward. There may come a time when you would really appreciate someone coming to visit you.

Moreover, there are thousands of younger people out there looking for some stability in their lives. Two award-winning programs to consider are Foster Grandparents and Big Brothers, Big Sisters. The beauty of these programs is they have wonderful introductory training programs to help you get involved, one step at a time. And if you can't find anything that directly interests you, call or email your local Area Agency on Aging (operating in almost every county in the U.S.) or conduct an internet search for an intergenerational volunteer opportunity near you.

Some programs now use online meeting platforms such as Zoom to build intergenerational relationships, so the connections can happen worldwide. Eldera (eldera.ai) is a global virtual village where generations come together to connect, learn from each other, have fun, and create a better future for all. Eldera connects kids around the world with vetted older mentors, one-to-one or many at a time, for weekly virtual conversation, story-time, and activities.[44]

Rob, an Eldera mentor, said of the program, "What inspires me the most is that during the time with my mentee, I become more childlike. I appreciate Eldera for transporting me back to someplace exciting and new and warm and memorable and familiar, all at the same time."[45]

# Building Intergenerational Relationships at Work

The 2015 movie *The Intern* cleverly captured longevity themes of the quest for purpose and the importance of intergenerational relationships. Robert DeNiro plays a seventy-year-old widower who had retired but came out of retirement in search of more purpose in his life. He takes a position as a "senior intern" at an online fashion business. After getting oriented to his new position and gaining the trust of the CEO, DeNiro's character provides good business advice to the CEO and becomes a mentor to her and others in management.[46] Marc Freedman of Encore.org notes that Chip Conley (cofounder of the Modern Elder Academy) "became a real-life version of the Robert DeNiro character in *The Intern*, who combines both a wise sage and one who also has a beginner's mind."[47] Conley, who created a successful hotel chain and sold it in his early fifties, was recruited by Brian Chesky, cofounder of Airbnb, so that the new upstart company could gain from Conley's wisdom and experience in hospitality. Airbnb did indeed benefit from his wisdom and experience, but Conley is quick to point out that he also learned a great deal from the young entrepreneurs at Airbnb. In intergenerational relationships, wisdom is shared, not simply handed down from older workers to younger workers.

This experience led Conley to write *Wisdom@Work: The Making of a Modern Elder*, which was published the same year he co-founded the Modern Elder Academy (MEA). For MEA, mid-life isn't a crisis; it's a calling, a calling that includes the importance of building intergenerational relationships.

# Building Intergenerational Relationships Where You Live

As mentioned in the first chapter, more people will be seeking to age in place, that is, in their current home. If this is your situation, you could find ways to connect to young people in your community through existing programs as described above. You might also consider a move to an intentionally intergenerational community.

Dr. Paul Irving of the Milken Institute wrote about several housing developments that bring together retirees and college students. For example, at Lasell Village on the campus of Lasell University in Newton, Massachusetts, older residents commit to studying with students in their teens and 20s. Likewise, the new Mirabella community at Arizona State University offers what it calls "a retirement experience sure to be unlike any other" that promotes physical, emotional, spiritual, social, and vocational wellness through intergenerational relationships. Irving notes that studies confirm the intergenerational connections and sense of purpose associated with these types of living and learning arrangements foster health, positive attitudes, and well-being.[48]

Because of the clear research available about the benefits of living in an intergenerational environment, Irving is critical of 55+ retirement communities that allow only those age 55 and over to live in them.

However, Marc Freedman notes that even if people choose to live in 55+ retirement communities, there are still opportunities for creating intergenerational relationships in the wider area. Freedman tells the story of Hal Garman, a retired minister in his 80s who moved into a community for seniors in a suburb of Washington, DC. He found intergenerational purpose and new relationships with younger people by recruiting more than 100 fellow residents to serve as afterschool mentors to local third, fourth, and fifth graders. In return, every week through the school year, the children visit the elders for a meal and activities."[49] If such a program isn't available to you, you can start one, or, as mentioned earlier, you can build such relationships through the internet with an organization such as Eldera.

Dr. Laura Carstensen, founder and director of the Stanford Center on Longevity, commented that the aging population has distinctive qualities to meet the needs of youth. Older adults are exceptionally suited to meet these needs in part because they welcome meaningful, productive activity and engagement. They seek—and need—purpose in their lives, and children need intergenerational relationships beyond their families.

Yet another benefit of establishing and enhancing intergenerational relationships is identifying some younger people to be on your Longevity Team (see Chapter 6), people who can provide the help that you need if you eventually experience a time of frailty later in life.

So, are you ready to start, or enhance, your intentional intergenerational journey?

# Questions and Suggested Activities

*Consider downloading the Longevity Planning Journal document from our website, LongevityRevolutionPress.com.*

**1** To which generation do you belong? Is the short description of your generation in this chapter accurate? What would you add or subtract?

**2** How is your generation different from that of your parents, children, or grandchildren?

**3** Outside of your family, how many significant relationships do you have with someone age 15 or younger? If you don't have any, please take a few minutes to list the reasons why in your journal. If you do have some, use your journal to list the benefits both you and the younger person are receiving from the relationship.

**4** Take the time each week to have a meaningful conversation with at least one person from a generation other than your own. Have these conversations for one month and decide if you want to continue. As you make progress, try to connect with members of all five of the generations that differ from yours and track what you learn in your journal.

**5** Make a list of all the places where you can interact with people from different generations—older or younger than yourself.

**6** Make a list of all the skills and experiences you would have to bring to a younger generation. What could you learn from them?

**7** What would you gain from a relationship with someone older than yourself? What could you share with them?

In order to improve the quality of your intergenerational relationships, you may wish to use a resource on intergenerational dialogue developed by Dr. James V. Gambone titled *Together for Tomorrow: Building Community Through Intergenerational Dialogue.*[50] This book is really two books combined. The first book helps the reader understand the importance of why we need more intergenerational thinkers and actors in an aging society (Chapters 1–4). The second book (Chapters 5–12) provides the reader with practical suggestions for improving intergenerational relationships, including how to organize Intergenerational Dialogues.

# 6

# Planning for Help Before You Need It

The underlying premise of this book is that you should expect to live a longer and more active life than you would typically expect to live. As you have seen, the research shows that most people living today will enjoy many more years than did their parents and grandparents. The research also shows that more of those years will be active and healthy years, the kind of years that make a longer life more enjoyable.

Nevertheless, for some people, there will be periods when activity is compromised, and, eventually, nearly all of us are likely to need help late in life. These needs come in many forms, and while you cannot predict them with certainty, you can prepare for some possibilities. Even though you may be decades from utilizing such help, we believe that intentionally thinking about and planning for those times of need will enhance your ability to stay in control if and when the time comes, thereby allowing you to maintain your independent lifestyle longer.

## Determining What is Most Important to You in Times of Need

The first step in this part of longevity planning is determining what is most important to you in a potential time of need. In Chapter 3, you were asked to think about your core longevity values, those that are deeply felt and long lasting. Establishing goals for times of need is an outcome of those deeply held values and your attitudes toward topics such as these:

- Remaining financially independent
- Maintaining control
- Maintaining privacy
- Leaving an inheritance
- Using government resources
- Involving family members in your affairs

Let's consider some examples based on these topics. For instance, your goals might include a desire to leave a financial legacy for your children, but, on the other hand, you might have the attitude that since you accumulated your financial resources, you should be able to fully use them to enjoy your life. Since you supported your children and got them started, maybe you think it's up to them to provide for their own comfort and financial security.

When it comes to using government resources as you age, you might believe that because you spent your lifetime paying taxes and supporting others, now it's time for you to collect any government support you qualify to receive. In contrast, it is equally possible that you believe you should be totally self-supporting throughout your life.

In terms of managing your personal affairs, you may want to keep them to yourself, share them with a small core team, or get the whole family involved. These are highly personal choices, and involving others in your personal affairs might mean giving up a level of control you are unwilling to cede. However, if you go this route, it could ultimately limit control over your situation because you are relying on one person—you—to accomplish everything. Although extreme openness can have its own risks, it has been our collective experience that choosing a trusted team of people to help with such matters is usually valuable.

University of Minnesota Professor Marlene Stum has developed a worksheet to help you identify your attitudes toward these types of issues. Called the Later Life Financial Security Goals Worksheet, it can be accessed for free on the University of Minnesota Twin Cities website.[51] The worksheet asks you to rate the level of importance of a series of statements related to the values and goals we have been discussing. It is an excellent, easy-to-use tool that will help you quickly determine your attitudes in these areas. Using it, you will find that your values and attitudes may fall at conflicting points on the continuum because there are simply no clear-cut answers. For example, perhaps you generally like to be in control, but you realize that for medical or investment decisions, you need assistance. In such cases, your attitudes and goals may shift as you decide that giving up some control will result in a better outcome. Either way, identifying these underlying attitudes helps you better understand the decisions you make. For instance, let's say there is a hypothetical person named Pat who took the quiz and discovered he had a stronger interest in leaving a legacy for his children than he expected, which helped him understand why he struggled to say "no" to his children's requests for financial support.

Again, some of your attitudes may conflict with others or change over time, such as maintaining privacy or involving your family in your personal affairs, but thinking about your goals and making sure they align with your values is the first step in outlining your future for the long term.

# Thinking About and Planning for Times of Need

Chapter 9 of this book will walk you through the steps of completing a Personal Longevity Plan based on your answers to the questions at the end of each chapter you have read. Part 2 of the plan covers this chapter: preparing for help when you need it and addressing the areas of housing, transportation, socialization, and legal/financial issues (including health care). An important facet of this piece of the planning process is assembling what we call your Longevity Team. Your Longevity Team is necessarily personal because these are the people who will support you in all aspects of your life during those times when your ability to be totally independent is compromised. To help you accomplish your goals, your Team members may work as individuals or as a group—perhaps both, depending on the situation. Your Team not only reinforces your strengths but also fills gaps in your knowledge and skills. Your Team may include family and friends as well as professionals, such as your financial advisor, who might also serve as a resource for others on your Team. The bottom line is that as you prepare for life during times of need, you must consider those who will help you along the way.

As we age, we clearly see that we get to control some aspects of life and influence others, but parts of our life simply unfold without our consent. Although maintaining independence and being in control are goals for nearly everyone, sometimes, as we age, things happen that threaten our independence. Suppose, for instance, that you consider staying in your current home the best housing option, so you make that part of your Personal Longevity Plan. This chapter asks you to consider what events could potentially jeopardize that outcome. Your children might move to a distant city, relocating the grandchildren you long to have nearby. Unexpected financial difficulties may make covering the expenses of home ownership impossible. Upkeep on the property might, over time, become more than you can handle. Declining physical capabilities might make it hard to execute the activities of daily life, such as climbing stairs or preventing falls in the bathroom.

The issue is this: Have you sufficiently planned to mitigate those potential obstacles? The remainder of this chapter discusses factors to think about as you address this question. While not exhaustive, it speaks to those issues we have encountered when working with our own clients to prepare for their future regarding housing, transportation, socialization, and financial/legal/health care matters.

# Maintaining Control and Independence in Your Home

The best way to maintain control and independence in your home is through simplifying the environment and lining up the help you need, as dictated by your goals.

Our hypothetical friend Pat has a 93-year-old neighbor we will call Tyrone, who has an extensive garden. Tyrone spends time every day planting, weeding, or watering. He loves doing it; it energizes him. But Pat also has a 40-something neighbor, let's call her Katie, who regrets having her much smaller garden because small as it is, she thinks it requires too much care. Clearly, Tyrone and Katie have different values and goals. Hopefully, by the time Katie is Tyrone's age, she will have figured out that she needs to foster those activities that give her energy and eliminate those that deplete it.

This understanding allows each of us to determine what tasks we want to do ourselves for as long as we can and what tasks we want or need to delegate to others. If you gain energy from mowing the lawn, by all means, mow the lawn, but if you do not, find someone to mow it for you or look for a home with a smaller or nonexistent lawn. In either case, determine what you would do if mowing the lawn becomes difficult or impossible. Even Tyrone, who is energized by working in his garden, needs to think about how to deal with the garden if his abilities change and he cannot keep up with it. Will he simplify it so he can care for it, find someone else to care for it, stop planting it, or move to a house without a garden? The same is true for any of the tasks associated with the upkeep of a home—shoveling, climbing ladders, painting, raking, etc. Advance planning keeps you in control of your choices.

In addition to considering the help you might need for the upkeep of your home, you may need assistance with the day-to-day tasks of living, such as laundry, food preparation, housekeeping, and personal care (bathing, dressing, hairstyling, and so on). Depending on your values and goals, the people you choose to provide these services might be professionals that you keep at arm's length—they provide a service, and you provide a check. Alternatively, these service providers could be family members or close friends, people with whom you have a more personal relationship. Of course, you could hire a friend or relative to do some of these activities and have both a personal relationship and a paycheck involved. The important thing to consider is your comfort level with these people because those who provide support for your personal and environmental care become members of your Personal Care Team, one component of your Longevity Team.

Whether you want to stay in your current home as you age or want to move to a different home, the planning process is similar. If you are staying, what physical changes to your home may be needed? If you are moving, what are the features you want or need in your new home? Do you enjoy entertaining, or is your home your refuge? Do you like to have overnight guests, or do you prefer that visitors stay in a local hotel? Do you have holiday or special occasion traditions you want to maintain? Do you have hobbies that require a special type of space? Do you own exercise equipment and need room to use it? By identifying the activities you most enjoy engaging in at home, you can make accommodations that allow for continuing them as long as possible.

Whether aging in place or moving, you may need to consider making renovations or accommodations to your living space. Renovations might include installing grab bars (particularly in the bath), changing to lever handles instead of doorknobs, or providing accessibility features (such as ramps or wider doors). If your current home lacks features you desire or need, such as one-level living, you must weigh the cost of making the changes against those involved in making a move. A related issue is reviewing the safety features of your home. While important at every age, personal safety grows in significance as we age due to the risk of more serious consequences should there be an accident. Therefore, you should install smoke alarms in every room and anti-scald controls for hot water, ensure that lighting is well distributed and highlights walkways and safety hazards, and remove or secure throw rugs to prevent slips and falls. In terms of cooking, position the tools and dishes you use most often in the easiest areas to reach and consider whether your oven's controls are located such that you don't have to reach across the burners to turn your oven on or off.

If considering the features of your home leads to the decision to move, your planning process needs to expand. Think about how close your new home would be to shopping, parks, entertainment, restaurants, and other types of services you regularly use—barber, dentist, clinic, etc. Obviously, no home or location is perfect, so consider your highest priorities and choose accordingly. At the same time, you need to pay attention to how convenient your location is to the members of your Personal Care Team. Whether you are reevaluating your current home or choosing a new one, most of the features discussed here will probably be available at several price points, so, if need be, work with your financial advisor to determine the affordability of the decisions you make.

These suggestions regarding housing give you the option of making adjustments now or waiting until any potential obstacles become more likely. Waiting affords you the possibility of discovering solutions that currently are not apparent or happily discovering that the obstacles you may have expected never materialize. But it is still helpful to plan because no one makes the best decisions when under stress or when time constraints don't allow you to explore all your options. Of course, if making some of these changes would improve your home or your lifestyle both now *and* in the future, why wait?

# Maintaining Control and Independence in Your Transportation

Most of us want to have a car in the garage so we can drive ourselves wherever we want to go, whenever we want to go there. However, by looking at other modes of transportation, we could possibly maintain our independence longer if driving becomes difficult.

Begin by surveying the transportation options available to you if you can no longer drive. How would you get the things you need? Besides long-distance package delivery services, such as the U.S. Postal Service, United Parcel Service, and Federal Express, there are many delivery options for groceries, meals, medication, household goods, and other necessities. If you aren't familiar with them, just ask someone younger than you are. That person is likely to know all the possibilities. If you prefer to go get what you need yourself, some of you will have mass transportation options, such as buses or trains, but you can also find personal, for-hire transportation services, including taxis, Uber, and Lyft. You might also consider local services provided by your church, community, or county. Finally, a member of your Personal Care Team may help you with transportation. Sometimes, all you need to do is ask, and others are happy to help.

The goal is to identify affordable, fairly easy ways to get to the services you need and people you most frequently visit: shops, restaurants, friends, church, doctors, movies/theaters/museums, hairstylists, volunteer locations, and so on. Once identified, take a test run using the other transportation methods, so you are comfortable using them before you are forced to use them. And don't forget that walking is a fabulous way to get around. The exercise will help you retain your transportation independence and your physical health.

Keep in mind that if the day ever comes when you need a walker or a wheelchair, you must make sure your chosen transportation methods can accommodate that need. If that includes relying on members of your Personal Care Team, make sure they are trained to assist you in and out of the vehicle and to break down your equipment, which they will need room to transport in the vehicle they drive. While not difficult to do, such training will make life easier for all concerned.

Finding ways to get around despite any physical limitations is critical to maintaining the independent life you want to lead and overcoming transportation hurdles avoids the feelings of dependence and isolation that occur when transportation options are limited.

## Maintaining Control and Independence with Your Socialization

The National Academies of Sciences, Engineering, and Medicine, in their study *Social Isolation and Loneliness in Older Adults,* reports, "Approximately one-quarter of community-dwelling Americans aged 65 and older are considered to be socially isolated."[52] If social isolation is a problem for people living in a community at the relatively young age of 65, think of the amount of isolation that could occur in the 30 or more years beyond that! Unfortunately, this social isolation can lead to the very health issues you are striving to avoid.[53]

Instead of allowing yourself to become disengaged from others, we urge you to take steps not only to maintain your current relationships but to build new ones. Many of us have formed relationships through our children's school-related activities, but before we know it, our children graduate and move away. We also form relationships at work, but then we retire, and those relationships fade. Even at home, it can be difficult to identify activities we enjoy doing with our spouses, much less find others who want to join us in those activities. You may find that you must initiate the social activity because others, though often happy to join you, will not take the initiative on their own. Nevertheless, being intentional about taking that initiative is vital to staying socially connected because finding ways to maintain your social life can literally be a lifesaver. If you find this difficult, join or form a group that will guarantee regular interaction with others and will simplify scheduling. Bridge clubs, book clubs, service clubs, coffee clubs, and lunch dates can all be set up on a regular basis and provide something to look forward to that will be consistently on your calendar.

Although the closest relationship most of us have is undoubtedly with a spouse, it's a standard joke that some couples struggle to adjust to the increased amount of time they find themselves together in retirement. For that reason, it is important to talk about the activities you will do together, activities you will do on your own, and activities the two of you will do with others. Whether the others are children, grandchildren, lifelong friends, or people who share a passion for activities you enjoy, finding ways to get out of the house and socialize is critical. Furthermore, establishing patterns of socialization, both individually and as a couple, will help you maintain those patterns in the unfortunate case that one of you passes on.

As you carry out the planning process for times of need, be aware that the separate parts of your plan are interdependent. For example, you need to consider socialization when making plans for housing and transportation. Make it as easy as possible to socialize, given your location and your available transportation options.

The various people with whom you plan to socialize, either individually or in groups, help give your life meaning and become members of your Social Team. For some, the Team may need to include an accountability partner or group, people who help you find a reason or a purpose for getting up in the morning and who encourage you to get out of the house and fulfill that purpose. As discussed earlier in the book, your purpose does not need to be earth shattering or life changing, but it does need to exist. When you get blinded to your purpose, others can help you see things from a different perspective, which is why thinking about and carefully crafting your Social Team is crucial.

# Maintaining Control and Independence with Your Financial/Legal/Health Issues

As a rule, most of us are protective when it comes to sharing information about our financial, legal, or health issues. In some ways this is understandable; in other ways it makes no sense. In reality, the more assets we have, the more we rely on others to do these things for us, including hiring business managers to pay our bills, attorneys to manage our affairs, and health care professionals to keep us well. What is important for all these areas is that they are handled in ways that, once again, match your values and goals, whatever your situation as you age.

Needless to say, handling your finances includes much more than getting the bills paid. It is critical that your money lasts as long as you do and that you have the appropriate legal mechanisms in place to conduct your affairs. At the same time, it is equally important that you do not leave this world having plenty of money but unmet dreams because you denied yourself spending opportunities that would have fulfilled those dreams. Your best life is one in which you live out your dreams while remaining self-sufficient. In short, you want to use your resources as effectively as you can, but you also want to organize your affairs to avoid creating a burden for those you leave behind.

In order to plan for your money to last, you should take a couple of steps to consider putting mechanisms in place to carry out your final plans. First, be sure to work with your financial advisor to draft a financial plan that creates a projection of your income and expenses over your newly anticipated longevity age goal to see if your money will last as long as you expect to live (see Chapters 1, 2, and 9). Obviously, a projection that covers several decades will not be exact, but it will be more exact than not running a projection at all. You will also want to make sure you have a margin of safety in the calculation. What if unexpected events mean that you must add five percent to your expenses? What if your expenses are even higher? Will you still have enough money if your expenses are 15 percent more than projected? You can decide, with your financial advisor, how much of a safety cushion is needed for your level of comfort, which is also based on your values and goals.

In reviewing the financial aspects of your retirement plan, consider your income sources as well as your expenses. Currently, Social Security can be claimed anytime between the ages of 62 and 70, and the claiming age does not have to align with your retirement age. It is often a better option to use savings or other resources to cover expenses while you wait for the optimum claiming date for Social Security benefits. Often, claiming Social Security between the ages of 68 and 70 produces the most lucrative results, but the decision must be based on several factors relating to your individual circumstances, including your other financial resources, your health, your marital status, and others. Therefore, working with a financial planner could be crucial for your success.

As you work together to create your financial plan, be sure to incorporate monetary expectations surrounding your housing, transportation, and socialization needs as well as the related teams discussed in this chapter. Determine the costs you can afford and the optimal timing of any changes you may plan. Determine whether your resources will meet your needs and how you will access those resources when they are needed. Your financial advisor can help you determine what changes need to be made to your investment portfolio to provide available resources for both short-term spending (three to five years) and long-term planning for late-life spending.

Once the projection is in place, rerun it every year or two to make sure you retain your margin of safety as time passes. Not all your assumptions will be accurate, and some of your expectations may not come to fruition. Regularly updating the financial plan allows you to make adjustments over time that will keep the projections in line.

Having a plan to make sure your money lasts, your next step is to put mechanisms in place to ensure your affairs are easily handled when you are unable to care for them yourself due to health, injury, or death. For this, you need the expertise of an attorney to develop an estate plan, that, at a basic level, includes wills, power(s) of attorney, and health care directives (see also Chapters 7 and 9). The legal documents included in your estate plan describe what will happen when you die, but they also provide protection by naming the people who will make decisions on your behalf if your capabilities are reduced to the point you are unable to make your own decisions. If you do not have an estate plan in place and become incapacitated, it will be costly to appoint someone to make decisions for you. Of course, an even bigger concern is that you may have no control over who that decision maker will be. Again, planning is the key.

In brief, the components of your estate plan contain specific instructions for your family. These components include:

1. **A will**—Your will provides instructions for passing on your possessions (your estate) to those you name as heirs and appoints a personal representative (or executor) to carry out your wishes.

2. **A power of attorney**—Your power of attorney specifies the person or persons you have chosen to execute legal and financial documents on your behalf if you are unavailable or incapable of doing so.

3. **A health care directive**—Your health care directive provides guidance as to your wishes and names your health care agent, the person who will make health care decisions for you if your physical or mental state is such that you are unable to make such decisions yourself.

Depending on the complexity of your affairs, many attorneys will also recommend that you create a revocable trust, which transfers your assets to a separate legal entity that you control and that simplifies transfer at your death. Other trusts or documents that are sometimes needed include a cabin trust, a special needs trust, or a limited liability corporation (LLC). We highly recommend that you consult an attorney who specializes in estate planning to cover these bases. If you do not have a personal attorney, your financial advisor will likely be happy to recommend one. It is easy to see why your lawyer and your financial advisor become essential members of your Longevity Team.

In addition to creating a health care directive to convey your wishes in the event of a health emergency, you should also consult your doctor(s) and insurance agent about planning for your care. Identify what long-term chronic conditions might be in your future and evaluate how you would cover the cost of treating or living with those conditions. Obviously, health insurance helps manage the cost of many acute and chronic illnesses, but you need professionals to help you evaluate whether your health insurance well suits your health needs. The people involved in providing your care comprise your Health Care Team, which may be small or large depending on your health and activities. Your Team may include a primary care physician, one or more specialists, a dentist, a personal care coordinator, and health-related insurance professionals in addition to your health care agent. Your Health Care Team might also include a trainer who assists you at the gym, a dietician who consults with you on enhanced nutrition (see Chapter 4), or an occupational therapist who strengthens your motor skills. Likewise, the Team could also include your running, biking, golfing, or walking club. Anyone who helps you stay healthy and active automatically becomes a member of your Health Care Team. As a bonus, these people also provide additional opportunities to socialize.

Just as with planning for your housing, transportation, and socialization needs when aging, maintaining independence and control in terms of your finances and health requires careful forethought and planning. However, unlike the other areas we have covered in this chapter, the issues of finance and health care most often require the expertise of professionals. We urge you to find professionals you trust and to talk with them honestly, openly, and frequently. As mentioned above, your financial advisor can be an excellent source for finding those who can help you navigate the difficult decision you need to make. For example, Raymond James has vetted other businesses that advisors can recommend to assist you with issues such as enrolling in Medicare, managing healthcare needs, aging in place, storing and sharing vital legal documents, and protecting against fraud. Other financial firms may provide similar services, so be sure to check with your financial advisor.

## Bringing the Plan Together

We have covered several facets of planning for help before you need it, but you may be wondering what that plan looks like in real life. Before we close, let's consider how another hypothetical person named Joann manages life in her home well into her 80s by having applied the concepts we discussed and by assembling an effective Longevity Team to meet her needs.

At 85 years old, Joann has realized for years that she can retain her independence and stay in her home longer if she asks for help when she needs it. Joann's hypothetical friend from church, we'll call her Margaret, drives her to services, making her a key member of Joann's Transportation Team. Margaret, although 86 years old herself, is a more confident driver and appreciates the company. Both Joann and Margaret have strong ties to their church community and typically attend services and other activities there at least four times per week, which makes Margaret a member of Joann's Social Team as well.

Let's say Joann has a son, we'll call him Gary, who owns a landscaping business and is handy, so he does yard work and takes care of household repairs for Joann. She still likes to putter around the yard, weeding and watering her flower garden, but it is nice to know that anything beyond that will be done by Gary.

During the winter months, Joann's neighbor clears Joann's driveway and sidewalk so she can easily get to her mailbox. Although Joann does not drive, she is able to walk quite well and helps another neighbor—who, at the age of 95, still lives alone—by bringing in his mail, tending his plants, and socializing with him. Taking on this role has given Joann a purpose for getting out every day. Joann's neighbors and her son Gary are members of her Personal Care and Social Teams.

Joann's eldest hypothetical child is a daughter, Michaela, who is a member of her Health Care and Financial Team. She coordinates medical appointments, provides transportation, participates in consultations with doctors, and helps to monitor health needs, including diet and medications. Joann has been fortunate to work with her physician, let's call him Dr. Brown, for 15 years, so they share a strong relationship and talk openly about Joann's preferences for care. Michaela also serves as Joann's agent for financial affairs and her personal representative. Although Joann still pays most of her day-to-day bills, Michaela and Joann regularly review income and expenses with Joann's financial advisor, who we will call Eleanor, to ensure everything is up to date. Eleanor takes care of Joann's investments and helps coordinate Joann's gifts to charity. She is also the one who introduced Joann to the attorney who drafted Joann's health care directive, power of attorney, and will.

Carlos, Joann's hypothetical accountant, introduced Joann to her book club. The 10 members of the group read a new book each month and gather over lunch to talk about it (or about other things, depending on how good the book is). Joann also has regular lunch dates with a group of women who have been friends since college. Having no agenda, they just talk about old times and wonder what the world is becoming. These Social Team members help keep Joann active.

As you can see, Joann has an extensive group of people around her who fill gaps in her knowledge and capabilities and who enhance her daily life. All of them are members of the various sub-teams that together comprise Joann's Longevity

Team. Some are paid, but many are friends and family who are just happy to help. By intentionally building a complete Longevity Team, Joann has access to the people, activities, and resources that allow her to lead a rich life, and she has no thoughts of slowing down. Wouldn't it be great if more people were like Joann?

# Questions and Suggested Activities

*Consider downloading the Longevity Planning Journal document from our website, LongevityRevolutionPress.com.*

**1** Rate the following goals on a scale of 1 to 5, with 1 signifying the goal is not important to you and 5 signifying it is extremely important to you. Consider refining your assessment by using Marlene Stum's Later Life Financial Security Goals Worksheet. If you are married, compare your ratings with your spouse's ratings and discuss any differences.

a. Remain financially independent

    1    2    3    4    5

b. Maintain control

    1    2    3    4    5

c. Maintain privacy

    1    2    3    4    5

d. Involve family members in my affairs

    1    2    3    4    5

e. Leave an inheritance

    1    2    3    4    5

f. Use government resources

    1    2    3    4    5

**2** What are the top three things your current home might need to allow you to age in place?

**3** How comfortable are you with alternatives to your personal automobile for getting around? Name specific options you would be comfortable experimenting with.

**4** Can you name five or more ways you are socially connected with others during the week? What ideas do you have for adding to your social circles?

5 Does your financial plan need a tune-up to account for your 100-year lifespan? What changes or issues do you want to discuss with your financial advisor?

6 Have you created a health care directive? If so, when was the last time you reviewed it?

7 Make a list of all the people who are currently part of the teams that will, together, become your Longevity Team. Make another list of people who do not currently help you in any way but that you would be comfortable asking for help should the time come when you need it.

# 7

# Leaving a Holistic Personal Legacy

Establishing and leaving a legacy has traditionally been viewed as planning for what will happen to your assets after you die. However, a holistic personal legacy is much more because it involves two more elements: 1) drafting an ethical will, and 2) creating a spirit legacy. An ethical will involves matters of the heart, the things you most love in life. It serves as a vehicle for writing down your values, beliefs, life lessons, and hopes for the future, including the people, places, and causes you care about. Similarly, a spirit legacy also involves matters of the heart rather than tangible assets, such as money or property; however, the word "spirit" is used very broadly. It involves not only what you may or may not believe about God or whether you belong to a specific faith community but also anything meaningful that you want to pass on as a story from your life experience. Daniel Taylor, the author of *Creating a Spiritual Legacy*, wrote, "Your life is not *like* a story; it *is* a story. And if any part of it is to have significance beyond you, this story must be told."[54] This is not to say that we are encouraging you to write an autobiography, but you are encouraged to select a number of stories that tell your spirit legacy. As you can already see, there will be an overlap between your ethical will—a heartfelt list of what is important to you—and the important life stories you decide to include. When you stop and think deeply about your legacy, isn't it true that your values (as stated in your ethical will) and the key stories that have shaped who you are as a person (as stated in your spirit legacy) are even more important than your financial and real estate assets or other personal possessions? Likely so. This is why you need to create a holistic personal legacy rather than just doing traditional estate planning.

# Sooner Rather Than Later

In the context of joining the Longevity Revolution, it might seem like there is no urgency for you to complete or even think about a holistic personal legacy. After all, if you're in your 60s and have three or four decades of life in front of you, why bother with this now? Aren't there other, more urgent things to do? Maybe, but there are three good reasons to do this sooner rather than later.

First, of course, is the fact that planning for healthy longevity doesn't mean that something can't happen to you in the near future. By completing your personal legacy now, you will have your proverbial "affairs in order," just in case. You will have the peace of mind that comes with knowing that if something tragic were to happen, you will have done the important work of creating your holistic legacy. When it's done, you'll feel good about it and be glad you did it.

Second, even though you may have a number of decades to live, creating your holistic personal legacy resonates well with what the Modern Elder Academy calls a "mid-life edit." Composing your ethical will and spirit legacy provides a current summary of what's important to you about your life when you still have time to add, subtract, or enhance items included in that summary.

Third, engaging in the reflection will ultimately bring more clarity and passion to the plan for flourishing longevity you will create when you get to Chapter 9. The introspection required to focus on the components of your ethical will and the stories of your spirit legacy should help you create and sharpen goals to guide the rest of your life. What part of your personal legacy at this point in your life do you want more of in the next phase?

What has been missing from your life experiences that you would like to build into your future? Indeed, as you engage in the important process of creating your holistic personal legacy, you'll reap the rewards for the part of your legacy you're still creating.

Consider this real-life example. Alfred kept the subject of his personal legacy on the "back burner" of his mind until something happened that gave him the motivation he needed to address it. Born in 1833 in Stockholm, Sweden, Alfred studied chemistry and engineering and became a very successful entrepreneur, holding 355 different patents, the most famous of which was the invention of dynamite.

It was 1888 when Alfred was prompted to take immediate action to shape his legacy. Alfred's brother Ludvig died while in France, but a French newspaper erroneously published *Alfred's* obituary instead of Ludvig's. Yes, Alfred had the unsettling experience of reading his own obituary! Even worse, the obituary condemned Alfred for inventing dynamite with the headline: "The Merchant of Death is Dead." The obituary read, "Dr. Alfred Nobel, who became rich by finding ways to kill people faster than ever before, died yesterday." Alfred was shocked to discover that this was how others viewed his legacy, but he also realized that it wasn't too late to create the legacy he wanted to leave. He revised his will, designating nearly his entire fortune for a new foundation: the Nobel Prizes.

Today, we all know that Alfred Nobel's legacy are the Nobel Prizes that exist in perpetuity for the purpose of honoring those with exceptional achievements in literature, science and medicine, and peace. As a result of this bold mid-life edit, the name Nobel is no longer associated with dynamite and death but, rather, with humanitarianism and philanthropy.

What about you? Are you seeing the value of creating a holistic personal legacy? If Nobel's story, the peace of mind, or the positive connection to longevity planning aren't enough to encourage you to take action sooner rather than later, perhaps there are specific obstacles in your way that need to be addressed up front.

# Obstacles to Creating a Holistic Personal Legacy

We anticipate that you might encounter three stumbling blocks that prevent you from embracing the importance and urgency of creating your holistic personal legacy. The first is thinking less of yourself than you ought. To be sure, most of us are not and never will be as rich and famous as Alfred Nobel, but personal legacies are for everyone, not just the rich and famous. Be assured of the value of your life to others. Your story and what you have contributed are vitally important to all those who know and love you, especially your family. Think about the ancestors you have seen in photos but never got to meet. Wouldn't it have been great if they had written down what they valued and recorded their significant life stories, leaving both as a legacy you could have drawn on all of your life? Why didn't they do this? Perhaps because, like you, they thought their lives were unimportant or too ordinary. Yet it's precisely the ordinary, everyday stories that shaped their lives that we wish we knew about. You can change that for yourself, your close friends, and your extended family. You can share your values, your beliefs, your life lessons, your stories, and your hopes for current and future generations so that they will have them to draw on, both now and long after you are gone.

A second potential obstacle to creating a holistic legacy is that the subject matter forces people to face their own mortality. In his famous book *Seven Habits of Highly Effective People*, Stephen Covey offered a powerful guided meditation to introduce the second of the seven habits, "beginning with the end in mind." He asks the reader to visualize driving to a funeral parlor. Once there, the reader approaches the casket, shocked to find that the funeral being attended is their own! Covey posed questions like those Alfred Nobel faced: What are the speakers at my funeral going to say about me? How am I going to be remembered? Regarding our own funeral speakers, Covey wrote,

"What kind of husband, wife, father, or mother would you like their words to reflect? . . . What character would you like them to have seen in you? What contributions, what achievements, would you want them to remember?"[55] Covey's exercise helps us face our own mortality but also helps us realize we have the power and ability to shape our legacy, so the end of our story turns out the way we want it to. Facing our own mortality can actually be life-enhancing if it serves as the motivating force for creating our personal legacy.

The third obstacle is simply pure procrastination. It's the "I'll get to it someday" attitude. Unfortunately, because someday is not an actual day of the week, someday never comes. There might be hundreds of Sundays, Mondays, Tuesdays, etc., in front of us, but there are definitely no somedays. Time is precious, begging us to be purposeful with the time that we have, even as we envision the potential for a leap in our longevity. Because the question of your personal legacy *is* important and involves much more than financial assets and property, the question for you is this: What day of this month will I start working on my holistic personal legacy? Having a specific answer to this question resolves the procrastination issue. Once you have a start date on the calendar and commit to honoring it, you are on your way.

# Creating a Holistic Legacy: Traditional, Ethical, Spiritual

For most people, creating a holistic personal legacy isn't about making as drastic a change as the one Alfred Nobel made. It's more about being motivated enough to actually get it done, but how do you go about doing that? The rest of this chapter will walk you through the three components of holistic legacy planning in an effort to encourage you to take the first step to complete this journey.

# 1) Traditional Legacy Planning

You likely already know the basics of traditional legacy planning because they were discussed in the previous chapter. Such plans typically involve a will or trust, and if you have retirement accounts, usually family members are listed as beneficiaries. Keep in mind that beneficiaries can also include charities, friends, or any other person or institution of your choosing. For those with a spouse or significant other, begin this process by talking to one another and then meeting with your financial advisor and an attorney. The attorney will draft a will and a trust, if that is appropriate, as well as other documents such as a power of attorney, health care directive, and health care power of attorney (see also Chapters 6 and 9). If you already have a will or a trust, you should review these documents every five years in case changes are needed.

As you establish or review your will/trust documents, consider how your beneficiaries are listed on your various retirement accounts. For financial accounts other than retirement accounts, such as brokerage accounts, ask your financial advisor to put a "Transfer on Death" (T.O.D.) on them. Similarly, at your bank, you can ask that a "Payment on Death" (P.O.D.) be established on checking and savings accounts. Most states also allow you to attach a legacy document to your home called a "Transfer on Death Deed" (T.O.D.D.). All of these safeguards allow your assets to pass to your heirs without going through probate. Again, be sure to also review the beneficiaries on any annuities or life insurance policies you have in case you want to make changes.

With respect to valuable personal property, itemize who gets what and include the list as an addendum to your will or trust. Bear in mind that sometimes certain things have more emotional than financial value to family members, so making decisions about these items may help avoid family conflict after you are gone. An excellent resource for having family conversations about these issues is *Who Gets Grandma's Yellow Pie Plate?*

*Workbook: A Guide to Passing on Personal Possessions* by Dr. Marlene Stum, who also created the Later Life Financial Security Goals Worksheet referenced earlier.[56]

## 2) Your Ethical Will

The second component of your holistic legacy is an ethical will, an expression of what is near and dear to your heart, what you have found to be important to this point in your life. Unlike a traditional legacy, an ethical will does not require hiring an attorney. It's something you write on your own. Even though you may have never heard of ethical wills, they are not new. In fact, the Hebrew Bible first described them 3000 years ago. At that time, they were transmitted orally, close to the time of death, but they can certainly be shared with family and friends while you are still here.[57] Barry Baines, a physician and author of *Ethical Wills: Putting Your Values on Paper* and *The Ethical Will Writing Guide Workbook*, defines an ethical will this way: "An ethical will is a way to share with your family and community your values, beliefs, life lessons, hopes for the future, love, and forgiveness."[58]

Given these basic parameters, we provide an example of an ethical will written by one of our coauthors, Dr. James V. Gambone. We hope you find it useful as a guide to writing your own ethical will.

## The Ethical Will of Dr. James V. Gambone

### My Personal Values

After 74 years of living in the United States and about three years living and traveling between Columbia, Mexico, China, Japan, Costa Rica, the Dominican Republic, England, Sweden, and Canada, I have developed some basic personal values that I hope make me a good person who contributes to the world. As I see it, these values are:

- Listening to what others have to say.
- Expressing compassion for those who have had fewer opportunities than me.
- Being honest in personal and business dealings.
- Keeping my word.
- Speaking out against injustice toward people, animals, or the environment.
- Recognizing that I am not perfect and not expecting perfection from others.
- Giving a full effort to all I am doing and expecting the same kind of effort from those who work with me.
- Respecting differences—knowing not everyone thinks, acts, or believes as I do.
- Being kind and friendly to strangers.
- Having the courage to be countercultural.
- Being a loving and caring husband, godfather, and dog dad.
- Believing cooperation is a higher value than competition.
- Walking my talk—trying to model what I talk about in my work.
- Being known as a person of integrity.

## My Hopes for Future Generations

I hope:

- We find a way to have peace with social and economic justice in every nation of the world.
- All human beings are able to develop whatever talents they have within them.
- We treat animals and all living things with the same respect we have for our own species.

- We treat the environment as a delicate ecosystem that enables all species to enjoy life.
- Hatred is replaced with love.
- People of the earth can get beyond the concept of the nation-state.
- All generations will show respect, caring, and cooperation for each other through personal contacts and relationships in the new information age.
- All religions and expressions of faith see each other as complementary and not competitive.
- Spiritual values become more important than material values.
- No person on this planet dies from hunger, insufficient housing, or lack of care.
- The true measure of our humanity becomes how well we treat those who are not able to take care of themselves.
- Every day is a new adventure in which we can help each other become better human beings.

**My Blessings for Future Generations**

I wish that all generations might claim the blessings of compassion, hope, love, reason, honesty, integrity, balance, belonging, risk-taking, a lively inner child, faith in something beyond the material, good spirit, longevity, high quality of life, solitude, health, good luck, well-being, charity, and humor.

**Life's Lessons**

Here are 10 life lessons I have learned so far:

1. I need to take care of myself and my family. If I am not able to do that, it is very difficult for me to take care of others.

2. I cannot change another human being. No matter how hard I try, people will change only if they decide to change themselves.

3. Positive reinforcements always work better than negative ones.

4. Never assume anything.

5. Not all issues are equally important to me. No person is capable of righting every wrong committed in the world. I must pick my causes carefully.

6. Love will ultimately win out over hate.

7. I live my life on the premise that most people are basically good.

8. It is important to have as many varied experiences as I can; otherwise, I will make decisions based on very limited personal knowledge.

9. Don't take things for granted—especially the people you love.

10. There is something beyond this life. That is what gives real meaning to my rather temporary—and sometimes painful—existence as a human being.

---

As you can see, an ethical will basically lists important personal values, hopes, beliefs, blessings, and life lessons. To be sure, the content of yours may be different from or similar to the example we've provided, but that's the point. This is to be *your* ethical will, not your spouse's or your parents', but yours and yours alone.

## 3) Creating Your Spirit Legacy

As mentioned at the beginning of this chapter, a spirit legacy is similar to an ethical will but with this important difference: a spirit legacy is about your important life stories. Writing about your life stories may seem like a daunting task, but it really isn't. Again, we are not suggesting that you write an autobiography. In fact, a spirit legacy can be as short or long as you wish. It is the quality of the stories you select to tell, not the number of words that is important. If you aren't a writer, a spirit legacy can also be done in the form of a video or an audio recording. If you decide to record your spirit legacy rather than write it, consider having your spouse or another family member interview you by simply asking you to share some important events in your life. Without writing down a single word, the stories you tell become your spirit legacy as they are recorded. Whether you choose to write your stories or do a video or audio recording, having a way to proceed is important.

To give this important part of your holistic legacy your best effort requires some solitude and some time for personal reflection. If you live by yourself, it may only require time to be intentional about this effort, setting time aside from what you normally do on an evening or weekend. If you are married or have a significant other and/or children living with you, finding time for solitude might be more challenging. Do you have space at home you can go to for some quiet time without interruption? Is this space good for personal reflection? If not, it might be better for you to schedule time away from home to reflect on your holistic legacy. Maybe you can schedule a weekend at a bed and breakfast. If that doesn't appeal to you or doesn't fit your budget, find a quiet coffee shop, go for a walk, or hike in the woods— anywhere you can reflect on some of your life stories.

Together, your traditional, ethical, and spiritual legacies create a holistic view of you and your life that those who love you are bound to appreciate and cherish. They eliminate any second guessing or wondering about who you were or what you valued when you are no longer here. There is truly no greater gift you can give.

# Questions and Suggested Activities

*Consider downloading the Longevity Planning Journal document from our website, LongevityRevolutionPress.com.*

Spend no more than a half hour to 45 minutes on the exercises for this chapter. The following questions are intended to "prime the pump" for writing your holistic personal legacy, but you'll likely need more time to complete it.

**1** Quickly assess where you stand with respect to traditional legacy planning:

**Yes    No**

❏    ❏    I have a will.

❏    ❏    My investment accounts and bank accounts are properly titled so that when I die, these assets will pass according to my wishes.

❏    ❏    I have someone I trust to be my durable power of attorney, and such documents have been drawn up and signed.

❏    ❏    Any life insurance policies and annuities that I own have the correct beneficiaries according to my wishes.

❏    ❏    I have a transfer on death deed (T.O.D.D.) for the house.

❏    ❏    I have decided how my personal property will be given away/disposed of after I die.

❏    ❏    I have a health care directive and a durable health care power of attorney.

❏    ❏    I have given the person who is my durable health care power of attorney a copy of my health directive and my living will.

2 The following questions will help you begin thinking
about the content of your ethical will. In your journal,
write brief answers to the following questions:

• What are your values? (Refer to the work you did in Chapter 3.)

• What are your beliefs?

• What are some key life lessons you would like to pass on
to others?

• What are your hopes for the future?

• Whom do you love?

• What are your thoughts on forgiveness?

**3** The following questions are meant to spark initial ideas for writing your spiritual legacy. In your journal, jot down brief answers, one or two words or a phrase, in response to these questions:

a. What two memorable stories from your childhood might you like to include in your spirit legacy?

b. What two memorable stories from your early adulthood might you like to include in your spirit legacy?

c. What two stories from middle age might you like to include in your spirit legacy?

# 8

# Mining Wisdom for Balanced Goal Setting

This chapter introduces sources of wisdom you probably don't even know that you have and encourages you to mine them as you start thinking about setting balanced longevity goals that will cover far more than finances. As always, you are ultimately striving to best answer the overarching question: **"How can I make my potential 100+year life the most fulfilling it can be?"**

## Sources of Wisdom

Virtually everyone is familiar with two sources of wisdom. The first is your Intelligence Quotient (IQ), typically determined by a standardized intelligence test. While there is disagreement over whether and how much a person's IQ can change over time, we all have the ability to learn more over time, so we have included accumulated knowledge as part of your IQ wisdom source. Most of you are also familiar with your second source of wisdom, your Emotional Intelligence Quotient (EQ). Although less common than IQ assessments, EQ tests measure your ability to positively manage the emotions that influence your behavior and decisions as you navigate the ups and downs of everyday life.

What you may not know is that you have two more sources of wisdom, a Curiosity Quotient (CQ) and a Transition Quotient (TQ). Your Curiosity Quotient (CQ) has to do with your ability to approach life with the desire to learn. Cognitive scientists suggest that your level of CQ actually predicts success in life equally as well, if not better, than your IQ or EQ, so it is obviously a great source of wisdom.[59] The more curious you are, the more you learn and want to learn, a cycle that keeps the mind active and fully alive. Your Transition Quotient, a concept taught by the Modern Elder Academy, demonstrates your ability to effectively handle significant life changes. The many transitions you will face over the coming decades, some welcome and some less so, make a healthy TQ indispensable for flourishing in the Longevity Revolution. Although seldom talked about, TQ is beginning to be recognized as an essential source of wisdom throughout the aging process.

As you become more and more aware of your various sources of wisdom, you will find that IQ, EQ, CQ, and TQ are dynamically and directly correlated. In other words, increasing one positively affects another. This is a relationship that can be illustrated in what we call The Wisdom Quadrants, shown below.[60]

# The Wisdom Quadrants
## A Dynamic Model of Holistic Wisdom

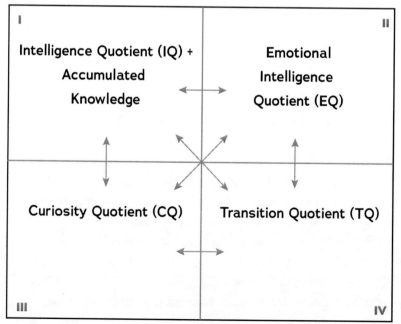

For example, the more knowledge you accumulate (using your IQ), the more curious you are likely to become. Likewise, the more curious you are, the more knowledge you accumulate. An increase in both your knowledge and curiosity makes for smoother transitions in life, thereby improving your TQ. By adding a healthy dose of EQ to productively manage your knowledge and curiosity and to become better at life transitions, you ultimately improve the overriding goal of this entire process: your ability to fulfill your life purpose(s) and enhance your core values. The Gestalt psychology principle of awareness is key to such growth. As you are more aware of how the Wisdom Quadrants impact your daily life and decision-making, the awareness itself produces growth. An excellent tool for capturing your insights regarding daily sources of your wisdom is the practice of journaling, something you have been doing as you make your way through this book.

As you consider ways to mine your four sources of wisdom during aging, you may find it useful to know that wisdom is now being studied from a scientific perspective. Dilip Jeste, M.D., a neuropsychiatrist who has spent more than 20 years studying aspects of wisdom and healthy aging, along with Scott LaFee, both from the University of California, San Diego, wrote *Wiser: The Scientific Roots of Wisdom, Compassion, and What Makes Us Good*. The authors say there is a biological basis to wisdom. Neurons in the brain fire in specific patterns in specific parts of one or more relevant neural circuits to produce behavior deemed to be wise.[61] Working with cognitive neuroscientist Michael Thomas, Jeste identified seven characteristics of wisdom, behaviorally expressed as:

- Acceptance of divergent perspectives
- Decisiveness
- Emotional regulation
- Pro-social behaviors (compassion and empathy)
- Self-reflection

- Social advising (giving relational and helpful advice to others)
- Spirituality

If you are interested, you can quickly benchmark your level of wisdom based on these seven characteristics by completing the Jeste-Thomas Index Assessment online at no cost. The instrument will provide a score for each item, which enables you to determine your strengths as well as areas you may wish to grow. Jeste and Lafee's book, *Wiser*, notes that such growth requires self-reflection, and they recommend both journaling and meditation to foster deeper introspection.

Being mindful of your sources of wisdom and their behavioral characteristics, you can now apply that knowledge as you prepare to set goals for the Longevity Revolution. As we said at the outset, it is time to look beyond traditional later-life goal setting centered on financial concerns. For you to live your best 100+year life, you are going to need an expanded yet balanced approach to this process.

# Balanced Goal Setting

If you think about the goals you set when you were younger, you would probably find that they centered on achievement— landing a good job, owning your own home, providing for your family, being recognized for a job well done, and so on. However, as we age, the Modern Elder Academy encourages us to move from that kind of achievement-based goal setting to goals that are soul-based. The difference is that achievement-based goals produce extrinsic rewards from without, such as admiration from others, while soul-based goals produce intrinsic rewards from within, such as the simple satisfaction of knowing you completed the goal and, in so doing, made yourself more complete as well. If you are at or nearing traditional retirement age, you have already "made it," so it's time to feed your soul, to allow yourself the joy of doing what you can do when there is nothing you need to prove to anyone. It's not that you need to abandon achievement in the decades to come, but that you give yourself permission to do those things that feed you as a person.

To that end, Dr. Shigehiro Oishi and Dr. Erin Westgate recently published a helpful article titled "A Psychologically Rich Life: Beyond Happiness and Meaning."[62] They suggest that living what they call "the Good Life" (and we call a fulfilling life) necessarily involves three components: 1) a *happy life* involving comfort, joy, and security, 2) a *meaningful life* involving significance, purpose, and coherence, and 3) a *psychologically rich life* involving variety, interest, and perspective change (e.g., consistently approaching your life experiences with a growth mindset and embracing new experiences, believing that variety truly is the spice of life). Oishi and Westgate go on to define one outcome for each of these three components of the Good Life:

1. The outcome of a happy life is personal satisfaction.

2. The outcome of a meaningful life is societal contribution [i.e., serving others].

3. The outcome of a psychologically rich life is wisdom born of a variety of life experiences.[63]

Although we consider wisdom both a source for effectively planning a fulfilling life as well as the result of having done so, you can see that the researchers' outcomes align well with what you have been reading in the previous chapters of this book. As you prepare to set goals for the Longevity Revolution, you must consider the proportion and balance of these outcomes in relation to your overall goals. In other words, you don't want to end up with goals that relate to only one or two components of a fulfilling life and, in the process, shortchange the other one or two. Oishi and Westgate make the cogent point that a happy and meaningful life can also be monotonous and repetitive without the variety that psychological richness provides. The easiest way to further understand their point is by looking at various examples.

Let's begin with the category of travel goals, which most people have on their list as they grow older. For a Minnesotan seeking to escape below-zero weather in January, a trip to the same warm, desert location year after year can be a happy experience, but not one that results in psychological richness because it lacks variety. In contrast, those who take yearly Road Scholar trips that offer what the organization's website calls "innovative . . . experiential learning opportunities" approach travel as an adventure characterized more by psychological richness than happiness.

Another example might be volunteering weekly at a local food shelf over a number of years. While serving others makes this a quite meaningful activity, the repetition means that it lacks the component of psychological richness, and it may also lack the component of happiness because so regularly seeing others in need can, indeed, be sad. Alternatively, volunteering for different Rotary International experiences, such as helping to build a medical facility in a remote area of the Amazon rainforest, clearly involves meaningful service, but it is more strongly characterized by the psychological richness that cross-cultural travel and the commensurate social interaction provide.

One last example would be limiting your book selections to any one favorite genre, such as mysteries, biographies, or historical fiction. Doing so may certainly result in a pleasurable, happy experience, but, again, it lacks the psychological richness that variety delivers. However, the same activity of reading a book could easily result in psychological richness by joining a book group that involves reading a wide variety of books, thereby broadening your perspective and providing stimulating social interaction through discussion.

The point is that when establishing goals for the Longevity Revolution, you will need to ensure that you have a balanced mix of happiness goals, meaningful-purpose goals, and psychologically enriching goals. The Good Life is within reach. You just have to plan—and dream—carefully, thoughtfully, and joyfully.

**"You are never too old to set another goal or to dream a new dream."** – Les Brown, motivational speaker

**"What is it you plan to do with your one wild and precious life?"** – Mary Oliver, poet

# Questions and Suggested Activities

*Consider downloading the Longevity Planning Journal document from our website, LongevityRevolutionPress.com.*

**1**  Go online and search for the Jeste-Thomas Index Assessment. After completing it, reflect in your journal about your scores on the seven characteristics of wisdom. What did you learn? If you have a spouse or partner, compare your scores, and discuss. Are there areas you wish to grow individually or together?

**2**  List at least five significant goals you met when you were younger. Were they primarily achievement-based goals, or were some soul-based?

**3** List at least five to 10 goals you would like to accomplish in the next five to 10 years. Then mark each with H for Happiness, M for Meaning, or PR for Psychological Richness. Do you have a balance among your goals? If not, how could you gain greater balance?

# Completing Your Personal Longevity Plan

You have reached the culmination of your journey—it is time to complete your **Personal Longevity Plan**. Doing so is a three-part process allowing you to pull together all that you have read, reflected on, and journaled since opening this book. Part 1 covers flourishing during the Longevity Revolution by asking you to set goals for living a longer, vibrant, fulfilling life. Using wisdom and mindset ideas from Chapter 8, you will incorporate content from the book and your journal entries for Chapters 1–5 to establish specific goals for your future. Part 2 covers planning for help when you need it, which involves reflecting on the chapter content and your journal entries for Chapter 6. Part 3 completes what you started to reflect on in Chapter 7: your holistic personal legacy. Once you finish all the activities in Parts 1–3, your Personal Longevity Plan will be complete!

Of course, the value of completing your Personal Longevity Plan is not simply to have it. The benefit comes when you implement your plan for the sake of thriving in the Longevity Revolution, so this final chapter ends with some important ideas to do just that.

# Personal Longevity Planning Part I: Planning for Flourishing in the Longevity Revolution

Reflecting on your potential extended lifespan will help you set life-fulfilling goals for the Longevity Revolution. As the late motivational speaker Jim Rohn said in his famous goal-setting workshops, "This [exercise] is not about what you think you can get. This is what you *want* if everything fell into place."[64] Those words of wisdom particularly apply to goals for joining the Longevity Revolution, but unlike Rohn's goals workshop, where participants generated up to 50 goals in about 20 minutes, you can and should take as much time as you need with this part of the process. Remember, time is your friend in the Longevity Revolution. As you move through the steps of Part 1, we encourage you to pause and review the mindset preparation material from Chapter 8. Doing so will provide inspiration for new goals as well as help you improve the quality of the goals you have already written.

You will discover that there are a number of steps involved in completing Part 1, but the estimated time it will take to complete all of them is about the time it takes to watch a movie. Since Part 1 will serve as the script for the "movie" about your life, it is well worth the time to complete each step with care. At the same time, keep in mind that you have already accomplished much of the needed groundwork through your reading and journal entries, so you are well on your way. For reference, the work you already completed is listed under the Groundwork headings below.

**NOTE: Before you begin, we suggest that you download the document "Personal Longevity Plan" from LongevityRevolutionPress.com for use in electronically completing your plan. For those who prefer to work with paper and pencil, we suggest that you copy Parts 1–3 of this chapter, so you have fresh copies of the planning steps for future use.**

## Step 1: Affirm Your Most Important Accomplishments

Begin by giving yourself credit for what you have already accomplished in life. (Yes, we know. Doing this tilts in the direction of an achievement-based life rather than a soul-based life, but this step helps underscore an "I can do it!" attitude for your goal setting. You've done it before; you can do it again.) These past accomplishments can act as a springboard for thinking about life-enhancing goals for your longevity plan.

List the five accomplishments you are most proud of:

1. _____

   _____


2. _____

   _____


3. _____

   _____


4. _____

   _____


5. _____

   _____

# Step 2: Define Your Planning Horizon

Groundwork:

Journal entries for questions #1 and #2 in Chapter 1 Questions and Suggested Activities

Exercise:

Remember that we have repeatedly said that aspiring to join the Longevity Revolution does not guarantee you will live in good health as long as you hope to. However, given what we now know, it makes sense to plan for that possibility.

Given the coming advances in aging science, if you could be both old *and* healthy, to what age do you want to live?

_____

What year will that be?

_____

Subtract the current calendar year from that future year to determine your longevity planning horizon and record it here:

_____

# Step 3: Include Elements of Lifelong and Long-Life Learning

Groundwork:

Chapter 1 section on Education

Exercise:

If you would like more information on long-life learning, read *The Emergence of Long Life Learning* by Chip Conley and Ingo Rauth and/or check out the online in-person workshops offered by the Modern Elder Academy (modernelderacademy.com).

What goals would you like to establish for yourself to promote lifelong learning?

_____

_____

_____

What goals would you like to establish for yourself to promote long-life learning?

_____

_____

_____

## Step 4: Advance Your Life's Passion and Purpose(s)

Groundwork:

Journal entry for question #4 in Chapter 1 Questions and Suggested Activities; Chapter 1 section on Purpose and Passion for Living in the Longevity Revolution

Exercise:

Do you have an overriding singular purpose in life, an ikigai? If so, what is it?

_____

_____

Do you have several purposes that comprise a purpose portfolio? If so, describe your purpose portfolio.

_____

_____

_____

## Step 5: Choose a Traditional or Nontraditional Retirement Path

Groundwork:

Journal entries for questions #1 and #2 in Chapter 2 Questions and Suggested Activities

Exercise:

a. If you prefer a traditional retirement (being done working for income by your mid-60s), have you checked with your financial advisor to see that you have properly planned for the cost of your goals? If not, specify the date by which you will call your advisor to make that appointment:

_____

_____

_____

b. If you want (or need) to work for income later in life, circle which of the following options you prefer:

- Continue full-time work beyond age 65 in my current position

- Cut back from full-time to part-time work in my current position

- Take a "bow" and come back for an encore career. Name that career:

_____

- Create a portfolio of activities that generate income. Describe these activities:

_____

_____

_____

## Step 6: Establish Goals that Advance Core Values

Groundwork:

Responses to questions #1–3 in Chapter 3 Questions and Suggested Activities

Exercise:

What are your *prescriptive* core values for longevity?

_____

_____

_____

What are your *descriptive* core values for longevity?

_____

_____

_____

# Step 7: Establish Goals that Focus on Healthy Longevity

Groundwork:

Journal entries for questions #1–12 in Chapter 4 Questions and Suggested Activities

Exercise:

Adopting and enhancing habits for healthy longevity are the most important goals you can establish, so specify the actions you will take for the sake of both your physical health and your brain health.

Physical Health:

_____

_____

_____

Brain Health:

_____

_____

_____

# Step 8: Establish Goals that Advance Intergenerational Relationships

Groundwork:
Journal entries for questions #1–7 in Chapter 5 Questions and Suggested Activities

Exercise:
Describe the social activities you want to be a part of going forward and specify the generation(s) of the participants you expect to include in those activities.

| Social Activity | Generation(s) of Participants |
|---|---|
| | |
| | |
| | |
| | |

## Step 9: Create Up to 50 Goals

Based on your responses to Steps 1–8, create a first draft of up to 50 goals for flourishing in the Longevity Revolution. As you begin, one goal after another may pop into your mind, but if you find yourself getting stuck, honor this by pausing and reviewing the previous Steps 1–8 to ensure that you include goals that directly relate to each step. For example, have you included goals that advance your purpose(s), long-life learning, core values, health habits for body and mind, and intergenerational relationships?

This wisdom exercise allows you to stretch your creativity and explore your imagination, but much like a potter throwing a pot, you will need time and care to refine the life goals you are shaping on your potter's wheel. Again, take the time you need.

If you need further inspiration to create up to 50 goals, return to these two questions as a mantra for flourishing longevity:

a. What goals do I want to complete that will make my potential 100+year life the most fulfilling it can be?

b. What goals would I want to complete if I had nothing to prove and everything to live for?

**Note: For now, ignore the BALANCE, YEARS, and COST columns to the right of the GOALS column.**

| # | Goals | Balance | Years | Cost |
|---|---|---|---|---|
| 1 | | H M PR | | $ $$ $$$ |
| 2 | | H M PR | | $ $$ $$$ |
| 3 | | H M PR | | $ $$ $$$ |
| 4 | | H M PR | | $ $$ $$$ |
| 5 | | H M PR | | $ $$ $$$ |
| 6 | | H M PR | | $ $$ $$$ |

| # | Goals | Balance | Years | Cost |
|---|-------|---------|-------|------|
| 7 | | H M PR | | $ $$ $$$ |
| 8 | | H M PR | | $ $$ $$$ |
| 9 | | H M PR | | $ $$ $$$ |
| 10 | | H M PR | | $ $$ $$$ |
| 11 | | H M PR | | $ $$ $$$ |
| 12 | | H M PR | | $ $$ $$$ |
| 13 | | H M PR | | $ $$ $$$ |
| 14 | | H M PR | | $ $$ $$$ |
| 15 | | H M PR | | $ $$ $$$ |
| 16 | | H M PR | | $ $$ $$$ |
| 17 | | H M PR | | $ $$ $$$ |
| 18 | | H M PR | | $ $$ $$$ |
| 19 | | H M PR | | $ $$ $$$ |
| 20 | | H M PR | | $ $$ $$$ |
| 21 | | H M PR | | $ $$ $$$ |
| 22 | | H M PR | | $ $$ $$$ |
| 23 | | H M PR | | $ $$ $$$ |
| 24 | | H M PR | | $ $$ $$$ |

| # | Goals | Balance | Years | Cost |
|---|-------|---------|-------|------|
| 25 | | H M PR | | $ $$ $$$ |
| 26 | | H M PR | | $ $$ $$$ |
| 27 | | H M PR | | $ $$ $$$ |
| 28 | | H M PR | | $ $$ $$$ |
| 29 | | H M PR | | $ $$ $$$ |
| 30 | | H M PR | | $ $$ $$$ |
| 31 | | H M PR | | $ $$ $$$ |
| 32 | | H M PR | | $ $$ $$$ |
| 33 | | H M PR | | $ $$ $$$ |
| 34 | | H M PR | | $ $$ $$$ |
| 35 | | H M PR | | $ $$ $$$ |
| 36 | | H M PR | | $ $$ $$$ |
| 37 | | H M PR | | $ $$ $$$ |
| 38 | | H M PR | | $ $$ $$$ |
| 39 | | H M PR | | $ $$ $$$ |
| 40 | | H M PR | | $ $$ $$$ |
| 41 | | H M PR | | $ $$ $$$ |
| 42 | | H M PR | | $ $$ $$$ |

| # | Goals | Balance | Years | Cost |
|---|-------|---------|-------|------|
| 43 | | H M PR | | $ $$ $$$ |
| 44 | | H M PR | | $ $$ $$$ |
| 45 | | H M PR | | $ $$ $$$ |
| 46 | | H M PR | | $ $$ $$$ |
| 47 | | H M PR | | $ $$ $$$ |
| 48 | | H M PR | | $ $$ $$$ |
| 49 | | H M PR | | $ $$ $$$ |
| 50 | | H M PR | | $ $$ $$$ |

## Step 10: Check Your Goals for Balance

Congratulations on completing your list of goals! Now, it's time to work with the column to the right of the goals column labeled BALANCE. This column reflects the discussion in Chapter 8, titled Balanced Goal Setting. The objective here is to edit your list of goals so that it reflects a balance between happiness goals (H), meaningful-purpose goals (M), and psychological richness goals (PR).

Although some goals may reflect more than one category, circle only one letter for each. For example, if a goal such as volunteering provides meaning but also makes you happy, choose the category that more accurately, not exclusively, reflects the goal. Also, note that the category for some goals, such as health-related activities, may not be readily apparent, but you should still be able to choose one of the three. For example, the goal of walking on a treadmill for 30 minutes a day is likely not in the PR category (i.e., psychological richness or "variety is the spice of life" category). That leaves either the happiness category (you truly enjoy the activity) or the meaningful-purpose category (you do it because good health is essential to fulfilling your purpose).

Exercise:

    a. To determine whether your goals are balanced, for each one, circle **H for happiness** goals, **M for meaningful-purpose** goals, or **PR for psychological richness** goals.

    b. When finished, count the number of items circled H, M, or PR:

        _____ H = Happiness Goals

        _____ M = Meaning Goals

        _____ PR = Psychological Richness Goals

    c. If you have roughly the same number of goals in each of the three categories, your goals are already balanced. If, however, one category has significantly fewer goals than others, consider adding goals to that category to create a better balance. The more balanced your goals that reflect happiness, meaning, and psychological richness, the more likely you are to live a fulfilling life.

## Step 11: Establish a Timeline for Completing the Goals

Exercise:

    a. For each of the 50 goals you wrote, estimate the timeline for completing the goal by writing 1, 2–5, 6–10, or 10+ in the YEARS column. If you know the exact year you want to complete the goal, please specify that year. Some goals, such as exercising or healthy eating, will never be completed, so write "ongoing" for those goals.

b. When finished, tally the number of goals you have in each of the categories:

_____ 1 year

_____ 2–5 years

_____ 6–10 years

_____ 10+ years

_____ Ongoing

c. If you have under- or over-loaded one of the time frames, consider adjusting your expectations. This is particularly important if you have too many goals in the 1 and 2–5 year categories. Don't pressure yourself by trying to complete too many goals too soon. As you complete individual goals, you can always adjust your timelines accordingly.

## Step 12: Estimate the Cost of Each Goal

The last column, COST, includes the symbols $, $$, and $$$ to represent the amount of money, if any, the goal will require for completion. Obviously, each person's view as to what constitutes a large amount of money will vary, so these estimates will be based on your particular financial situation.

Exercise:
a. If completing the goal will cost no money, leave the COST column blank. If, given your financial resources,

the goal will cost what you consider a small amount of money, circle $. If the goal will cost a moderate amount of money, circle $$. If the goal will be quite expensive, circle $$$.

b.  Bring the list of goals that you anticipate being quite expensive to your financial advisor so you can discuss them.

## Optional Step: Blend Your Goals with Your Partner's

Exercise:
Although you will complete some goals by yourself, those of you who are partnered will find that other goals, perhaps many, will involve your spouse or life partner as well. Given that, take whatever time you need to discuss and blend your goals, timelines, and expenses as needed.

# Personal Longevity Planning Part 2: Preparing for Help When Needed

The MIT AgeLab, in conjunction with Hartford Funds, has posed three simple but excellent questions regarding planning for help when the time comes that you need it.

- "Who will change my light bulbs?" [i.e., Do I have a plan for maintaining my home?]

- "How will I get an ice cream cone?" [i.e., Do I have adequate transportation to go where I want to go when I want to go?]

- "Who will I have lunch with?" [i.e., Do I have a social network of friends?][65]

As you can see, these three questions relate to what you read in Chapter 6, and they reflect the work you will do in Part 2 of this process. As stated earlier, if you are healthy and in your 50s or 60s, you may not need help for some decades to come, but it is still important to begin thinking through what you want to do and whom you want to include in your Longevity Team when you actually do need help.

### Groundwork:
Journal responses to Chapter 6 Questions and Suggested Activities

### Exercise:
Aligning your responses with the goals you set in Part 1 of your Personal Longevity Plan, answer the questions below.

  a. Given your current housing situation, consider the following:

- How many more years do you anticipate living in your current home?

    _____

- Are there any renovations you want to make now to prepare for aging in place? If so, list them:

    _____

    _____

    _____

- List all the people you might want to have on your Personal Care Team in order to stay in your home.

  _____

  _____

  _____

- If you did move, what kind of home(s) would you want? Circle all that apply.

  Single-family home

  Townhome

  Condominium

  Apartment

  55+ Community

  Assisted-living

  Other, specify _____

b. What forms of transportation are you willing to use beyond your own car?

  _____

  _____

  _____

c. Whom do you want to include on your Transportation Team?

_____

_____

_____

d. How do you plan to socialize on a weekly basis?

_____

_____

_____

e. Who are the primary members of your Social Team?

_____

_____

_____

f. List any actions you know you need to take to tend to your financial, legal, or healthcare needs and your timeline for completing them.

Action                          Timeline

_____

_____

_____

g. Name those people you want to include on your comprehensive Longevity Team to meet your financial, legal, and healthcare needs.

_____

_____

_____

# Personal Longevity Planning Part 3: Completing Your Holistic Personal Legacy

As discussed in Chapter 7, there are three parts to establishing a holistic personal legacy: traditional estate planning, an ethical will, and a spirit legacy. All three will be addressed as you complete this final part of your Personal Longevity Plan.

## Traditional Estate Planning

Groundwork:
Responses to question #1 in Chapter 7 Questions and Suggested Activities

Exercise:
Set a date for making an appointment with an attorney and/or completing any legal issues of traditional legacy planning that are still outstanding (i.e., all the "no" boxes you checked in response to #1 of Questions and Suggested Activities, Chapter 7).

Issue needing attention                    Timeline

_____

_____

_____

# Ethical Wills

## Groundwork:

Response to #2 in Chapter 7 Questions and Suggested Activities section; Chapter 7 section on Ethical Wills and the sample provided

## Exercise:

If you wish to delve deeper into the subject before writing your own ethical will, read Barry Baines' *The Ethical Will Writing Guide Workbook.*

a. Make an appointment with yourself for a two- to four-hour mini-retreat to complete your ethical will. Record the details below. When complete, attach your ethical will to this document.

   Date              Time                        Place

   _____


b. Name the loved ones you wish to share your ethical will with and schedule a time to do that.

   Names                        Occasion/Date for Sharing

   _____

   _____

   _____

## Spirit Legacy

Groundwork:

Response to #3 in Chapter 7 Questions and Suggested Activities; Chapter 7 section on spirit legacies

Exercise:

For more information, read Daniel Taylor's *Creating a Spiritual Legacy: How to Share Your Stories, Values, and Wisdom.*

a.  Schedule a weekend or a series of evenings to complete your spirit legacy, preferably in the next two months. Record the details below.

| Date | Time | Place |
|------|------|-------|
|      |      |       |

b.  Commit to a time and method (e.g., orally, recorded, in writing) for sharing your life stories with loved ones.

| Loved One's Name | Date | Method |
|------------------|------|--------|
|                  |      |        |
|                  |      |        |
|                  |      |        |

# Implementing, Monitoring, and Editing Your Personal Longevity Plan

Congratulations on completing your Personal Longevity Plan! Now you'll want to put it to good use, so we have tips for making the most of all the work you have done.

First, unless you already have a life coach or a business coach, your financial advisor may be in the best position to serve as your Longevity Coach. This new coaching relationship involves much more than making sure some money from your investment accounts shows up each month to supplement your Social Security income for retirement. As your longevity coach, your financial advisor should put your Personal Longevity Plan at the center of your financial advisory relationship, with the aim of helping you complete the longevity goals that require more substantial amounts of money to achieve.

Second, your advisor-coach should integrate your goals with traditional financial planning practices. Together, you may review your current financial position, risk management, investments, taxes, retirement planning, and estate planning. These "tried and true" financial planning practices directly support your Personal Longevity Plan because they interconnect with your new goals as a participant in the Longevity Revolution.

Third, as you complete the goals in your Personal Longevity Plan, you and your advisor-coach should monitor financial progress toward meeting your longer-term goals and help you with what the Modern Elder Academy calls "mid-life editing." In other words, your advisor-coach may celebrate with you as goals are met and help you adjust timelines and establish new goals for the years and decades to come. Your advisor-coach may run "what if" funding scenarios and test them with a computer program to determine their likelihood of meeting the financial costs of your future goals.

To help assist in this process, we have provided a Financial Advisor-Client Checklist to be used for the reviewing and mid-life editing process. As you work your way through the following grid, mark each item as **Complete – C** (the item is well in place), **Incomplete – I** (the item needs work or is deficient in some way), or **Needs Discussion – ND** (the item has yet to be addressed in a client/advisor session). Don't forget to update the grid as you participate in regularly scheduled reviews.

| Category | Item | C | I | ND |
|---|---|---|---|---|
| Financial-Related | Taxable Investment Accounts | | | |
| | Tax-Deferred Investment Accounts | | | |
| | Non-Taxed Investment Accounts | | | |
| | Cash Reserve | | | |
| | Business Assets | | | |
| | Real Estate | | | |
| | Asset Protection | | | |
| | Income Producing Assets | | | |
| Mortgage/Loans | Home Mortgage | | | |
| | Auto Loan | | | |
| | Business Loan | | | |
| | Credit Cards | | | |
| | Other Debt | | | |
| Protection/Insurance | Life Insurance | | | |
| | Long-term Care Insurance | | | |
| | Property Casualty Insurance | | | |
| | Personal Liability Insurance | | | |
| | Continuing Care Community | | | |
| | Health Insurance and Medicare Planning | | | |
| Income | Social Security Benefits | | | |
| | Pension Benefits | | | |
| | Other Income Streams | | | |
| Expenses | Monthly & Other Expenses | | | |
| Testing Scenarios | Premature Death | | | |
| | Extraordinary Longevity | | | |
| | Extraordinary Health Expenses | | | |
| Tax Reduction | Impact of RMD (Required Minimum Distribution) | | | |
| | Roth Conversions | | | |
| | Charitable Giving | | | |
| | Gifts to Family | | | |
| | Impact of Property Taxes | | | |

| Category | Item | C | I | ND |
|---|---|---|---|---|
| Estate Plan | Will | | | |
| | Power of Attorney, Durable | | | |
| | Health Care Directive and Health Care Agent | | | |
| | Trust Agreements | | | |
| | Asset Protection | | | |
| | Legacy Planning | | | |
| | Support for Dependents | | | |
| | Plans for Charitable Intentions | | | |
| | Title Changes Needed for Estate Plan | | | |
| | Discussed Overall Estate Plan with Agents | | | |
| | Ethical Will/Spirit Legacy | | | |
| | Organize Documents and Communicate with Agents | | | |

# Afterword

In the first chapter of this book, we quoted Dr. Joseph Coughlin of the MIT AgeLab, who said, **"We might want to start talking about longevity planning, rather than retirement planning."** We have, indeed, started talking about longevity planning rather than retirement planning and hope that, in so doing, we have inspired financial advisors and clients alike to embrace the call to *Join the Longevity Revolution* and create Personal Longevity Plans for themselves. If aging science progresses like the research shows that it will, the predictions made in this book will be realized by more people than we could ever imagine, affording them extra decades of healthy, fulfilling living.

We have tried our best to make you think by provoking your imagination and providing practical tools to help you plan for the Longevity Revolution, but as the saying goes, the only time "success" comes before "work" is in the dictionary. You will need to take concrete actions to fully participate in this new age of longevity.

We realize that some of these actions may be outside your comfort zone; they certainly were for the three of us. But going beyond our individual comfort zones makes us stronger, more flexible, and more successful human beings. Winston Churchill assured us that "success is not final; failure is not fatal; it is the courage to continue that counts." Those who have read this book and taken steps to complete a Personal Longevity Plan need not worry about courage. You clearly have the courage, fortitude, and motivation to continue this journey on your own.

As authors of this book, we thank all who have made this journey with us and wish each of you a healthy, flourishing, fulfilling 100+year life in the Longevity Revolution! We continue the journey with you and hope that this book has given you the best start possible.

– Brad Jenson, John Comer, and James Gambone

# About the Authors

Rev. Bradley C. Jenson, CFP®, CIMA®, AIF®, CAP®

Brad, a graduate of St. Olaf College and Luther Seminary, served as a youth director, hospital chaplain, and Lutheran pastor until 2002. Although he maintains his clergy credentials, he no longer sensed a call to serve as a parish pastor and transitioned to a position as a financial advisor, where he now has over 20 years of experience. Since 2009, he has served as a financial advisor and CERTIFIED FINANCIAL PLANNER TM (CFP®) professional with Lake Superior Financial Services, Inc., Duluth, Minnesota. *(Securities offered through Raymond James Financial Services, Inc. Member FINRA/SPIC. Lake Superior Financial Services, Inc. is not a registered broker/dealer and is independent of Raymond James Financial Services.)*

Brad understands his purpose in life as encompassing a portfolio of vocations or callings: (1) a relational purpose to be Jill's husband, her life partner; (2) a professional purpose to serve as a financial advisor whose primary focus is to help others with, and to write about, the longevity planning process; and (3) a theological purpose to research and write on spiritual-theological topics.

His interest in writing led to contributing a number of columns on longevity for Rethinking65.com, including a new series titled "Thought Leaders in Longevity." Brad has also published several articles in theological journals and coauthored *The Essential Bible: A Summary of the Major Stories* (2011) and *Luther and Bach on the Magnificat: For Advent and Christmas* (2015).

As a financial advisor, Brad holds the following credentials: CERTIFIED FINANCIAL PLANNER™, Certified Investment Management Analyst®, Accredited Investment Fiduciary®, and Chartered Advisor in Philanthropy®. He continues lifelong learning to maintain these credentials.

In pursuit of long-life learning, Brad is a Corazón Member of the Modern Elder Academy. In a spirit of gratitude for what MEA has contributed to his life, Brad dedicates his work on this book to the faculty and staff of the Modern Elder Academy, to his "compadres" in the MEA "We Are Complete" cohort, and to the entire MEA global community.

Regarding his core value of healthy longevity, Brad's goal is to live to the age of 110. He intends to cut back to part-time work when he turns 95 in 2051 and to continue working for the rest of his life.

Brad is a member of the Investments & Wealth Institute, the Financial Planning Association, the MITAgeLab's PLAN (i.e., Preparing for Longevity Advisory) Network, and the Duluth Harbortown Rotary Club.

# John M. Comer, CFP®

John Comer is a financial advisor with McNellis & Asato, Ltd., in Bloomington, Minnesota. *(Securities offered through Raymond James Financial Services, Inc. Member FINRA/SPIC. McNellis & Asato, Ltd. is not a registered broker/dealer and is independent of Raymond James Financial Services.)* He brings to his practice broad experience in financial planning, investment management, banking, marketing, product development, and communication. A CERTIFIED FINANCIAL PLANNER™ professional since the early 1990s, John is excited about helping financial advisors find ways to enhance the lives of their clients.

One of the ways John helps advisors help their clients is by teaching CFP® candidates "Retirement Planning & Employee Benefits" and volunteering with the Financial Planning Association. John's direct work in coordinating advisor support of financial capability training earned him the FPA Heart of Financial Planning Award.

Through work with the FPA, John met and formed a working group to explore longevity planning. Representatives of the Minnesota Department of Commerce, AARP Minnesota, the Minnesota Elder Justice Center, and the University of Minnesota

College of Education and Human Development joined John in developing a process that helps clients plan for their 100+year life. *Join the Longevity Revolution* will help the insights of this group reach a wider audience.

In addition, John is a member of MIT Agelab's PLAN network and a guest columnist for Rethinking65.com.

John is also active in the community. He serves in leadership roles at his church and at a local nonprofit that works to prevent child abuse and provides therapy to children who have suffered abuse. He also volunteers with local organizations that support financial capability, particularly in youth.

Personally, John enjoys running, canoeing, hiking, reading, learning, and contributing. However, he realizes that he does not engage in those activities more often because he so enjoys spending time with his wife, Donna, in whatever she is doing.

You can learn more about John M. Comer at McNellisAsato.com.

## James V. Gambone, Ph.D.

James Gambone prides himself on being a living model of what it means to have a successful, multi-portfolio career, being actively engaged in the work he loves long after a typical retirement age. He says, "Why should I stop doing something that provides meaning and happiness in my life?" As a social entrepreneur and business owner for more than 30 years, he has been a published author, educator, speaker, workshop leader, consultant, and media producer.

Jim wrote *ReFirement®: A Boomers Guide to Life After 50* almost 20 years ago. Now in its 6th printing, under the title *ReFire® Your Life*, the book has inspired people to take a deeper look at the Longevity Revolution.

Jim has written seven other books, his most recent being *Ride the Wild Pony and Other Stories From 57 Steuben Street*, which documents the first five years of his life when he lived in a Pittsburgh tenement with his mother, father, aunt, uncle, and his Polish grandmother—the first woman moonshiner and numbers bookie in the city. He is now working on his first novel, *The Immortal David Russell: A Roadmap to Eternity*.

Dr. Gambone is a part-time graduate professor of Public Health, teaching online for the past 11 years, and has served as a dissertation chair for 46 successful doctoral candidates. He is a respected expert and keynote speaker, nationally and internationally, on generational and intergenerational relationships.

He has also been an award-winning multimedia writer, producer, director, and distributor for over 30 years. His most recent production, *The Life and Loves of Sinclair Lewis* (2021), is streaming on the Sinclair Lewis Foundation website: sinclairlewisfoundation.org/life-and-loves

Over the past three years, Jim has taken up abstract painting with a small group called "The CathArtists," using alcohol inks as his medium. He painted a monthly history of the COVID pandemic, starting in January 2020 and continuing through 2022. Jim enjoys golfing, biking, and hanging out with his creative wife, Wendy, and their amazing dog, Willa.

You can learn more about James V. Gambone and his multi-portfolio career at pointsofviewinc.com.

# Further Resources

What follows is a list of resources for the Longevity Revolution that will deepen your longevity knowledge and further your journey in the Longevity Revolution. The order of the categories and resources generally reflects the order of chapters in the book. Some resources relate to more than one chapter, so they appear in more than one category.

## Longevity and its Potential

Barzilai, Nir. *Age Later: Health Span, Life Span, and the New Science of Longevity*. New York: St. Martin's Press, 2020.

Carstensen, Laura. *A Long Bright Future: Happiness, Health, and Financial Security in an Age of Increased Longevity*. New York: Public Affairs, 2011.

Cohen, Gene D. *The Mature Mind: The Positive Power of the Aging Brain*. New York: Basic Books, 2005.

Coughlin, Joseph F. *The Longevity Economy: Unlocking the World's Fastest-Growing, Most Misunderstood Market*. New York: Public Affairs, 2017.

Dixon, Anna. *The Age of Ageing Better?: A Manifesto For Our Future*. London: Green Tree, 2020.

Dychtwald, Ken, and Robert Morison. *What Retires Want: A Holistic View of Life's Third Age*. Hoboken, NJ: Wiley & Sons, 2020.

Gambone, James V. *ReFire® Your Life! A Guide for Those Who Can't Retire—Or Don't Want To*. Crystal Bay, MN: Elder Eye Press, 2011.

Gratton, Lynda, and Andrew Scott. *The 100-Year Life: Living and Working in an Age of Longevity*. London: Bloomsbury Publishing, 2020.

Harrison, Robert Pogue. *Juvenescence: A Cultural History of Our Age*. Chicago: University of Chicago Press, 2014.

Irving, Paul H. *The Upside of Aging: How Long Life is Changing the World of Health, Work, Innovation, Policy, and Purpose*. Hoboken, NJ: Wiley, 2014.

Levitin, Daniel J. *Successful Aging: A Neuroscientist Explores the Power and Potential of Our Lives*. New York: Dutton, 2020.

Levy, Becca. *Breaking the Age Code: How Your Beliefs About Aging Determine How Long & Well You Live*. New York: William Morrow, 2022.

Mercer. *Redesigning Later Life*, 2019. https://www.mercer.com/content/dam/mercer/attachments/private/gl-2020-6010715-mn-next-age-redesigning-later-life-mercer.pdf.

Miller, Lisa. *The Awakened Brain: The New Science of Spirituality and Our Quest for an Inspired Life*. New York: Random House, 2021.

Roizen, Michael F., Peter Linneman, and Albert Ratner. *The Great Age Reboot: Cracking the Longevity Code for a Younger Tomorrow*. Washington, D.C.: National Geographic, 2022.

Scott, Andrew J., and Lynda Gratton. *The New Long Life: A Framework for Flourishing in a Changing World*. London: Bloomsbury Publishing, 2020.

Sinclair, David A., with Michael D. LaPlante. *Lifespan: Why We Age and Why We Don't Have To*. New York: Atria, 2019.

Stanford Center on Longevity. "The New Map of Life," Extended Report, April 2022, https://longevity.stanford.edu/the-new-map-of-life-full-report/.

Zweig, Connie. *The Inner Work of Age: Shifting from Role to Soul*. Rochester, VT: Park Street Press, 2021.

## Long-Life and Lifelong Learning, Change, and Transitions

Conley, Chip, and Ingo Rauth, *The Emergence of Long Life Learning*. https://longlifelearning.education/.

Dweck, Carol S. *Mindset: Changing the Way You Think to Fulfill Your Potential*. New York: Random House, 2006.

Horwitz, Ilana M., and Mitchell L. Stevens, "Reimagining Education for a New Map of Life," November 16, 2021. https://longevity.stanford.edu/the-new-map-of-life-report/#1637124315004-b149a6e6-23ec.

Feiler, Bruce. *Life is in the Transitions: Mastering Change at Any Age*. New York: Penguin Press, 2020.

Hamaoui, Jeff, and Kari Henley. *The Anatomy of a Transition*, Modern Elder Academy, 2021. https://www.modernelderacademy.com/.

Milkman, Katie. *How to Change: The Science of Getting from Where You Are to Where You Want to Be*. New York: Penguin, 2021.

Vanderbilt, Tom. *Beginners: The Joy and Transformative Power of Lifelong Learning*. New York: Alfred A. Knoff, 2021.

## Passion, Purpose, Happiness, and Self-Actualization

Brooks, Arthur. *From Strength to Strength: Finding Success, Happiness, and Deep Purpose in the Second Half of Life*. New York: Portfolio/ Penguin, 2022.

Buettner, Dan. *The Blue Zones of Happiness: Lessons From the World's Happiest People*. Washington, D.C.: National Geographic, 2017.

Conley, Chip. *Emotional Equations: Simple Steps for Creating Happiness + Success in Business + Life*. New York: Atria, 2012.

Cope, Stephen. *The Great Work of Your Life: A Guide for the Journey to Your True Calling*. New York: Bantam, 2012.

Diener, Ed, and Robert Biswas-Diener. *Happiness: Unlocking the Potential and Mysteries of Psychological Wealth*. Malden, MA: Blackwell Publishing, 2008.

Dychtwald, Ken. *Radical Curiosity: One Man's Search for Cosmic Magic and a Purposeful Life*. Los Angeles: Unnamed Press, 2021.

Gaisford, Cassandra. *How to Find Your Passion and Purpose: Four Easy Steps to Discover a Job You Want and Life the Life You Love*. Santa Fe: Blue Giraffe Press, 2017.

Gaisford, Cassandra. *Passion Workbook*. https://www.cassandragaisford.com/wp-content/downloads/find-your-passion-eBook.pdf.

Gambone, James V. *ReFire® Your Life! A guide for those who can't retire – or don't want to*. Crystal Bay, MN: Elder Eye Press, 2011.

Honoré, Carl. *Bolder: How to Age Better and Feel Better About Aging*. Toronto: Vintage Canada, 2018.

Jenkins, Patrice. *What Will I Do All Day?: Wisdom to Get You Over Retirement and on with Living!* New Providence, NJ: Bowker, 2022.

Kaufman, Scott Barry. *Transcend: The New Science of Self-Actualization*. New York: TeacherPerigee, 2021.

Leider, Richard J. *The Power of Purpose: Find Meaning, Live Longer, Better*. 3rd Edition. Oakland: Berrett-Koehler Publishers, 2015.

Leider, Richard J., and David A. Shapiro. *Who Do You Want to Be When You Grow Old?: The Path of Purposeful Aging*. Oakland: Berrett-Koehler Publishers, 2021.

The Purpose Exchange. https://www.thepurposexchange.com/.

Secretan, Lance. *The Spark, The Fire, and the Torch: Inspire Self. Inspire Others. Inspire the World*. Caledon, ONT: The Secretan Center, 2010.

Seligman, Martin E.P. *Flourish: A Visionary New Understanding of Happiness and Well-Being*. New York: Atria Books, 2012.

Tolle, Eckhart. *A New Earth: Awakening to Your Life's Purpose*. New York: Penguin, 2016.

Waxman, Barbara. *The Middlescence Manifesto: Igniting the Passion of Midlife*. Kentfield, CA: The Middlescence Factor, 2016.

## Work

Alboher, Marci. *Encore Career Handbook: How to Make a Living and a Difference in the Second Half of Life*. New York: Workman Publishing, 2013.

Bolles, Richard N. *What Color is Your Parachute? 2022*. Berkeley: Ten Speed Press, 2021.

Conley, Chip. *Wisdom@Work: The Making of a Modern Elder*. New York: Currency, 2018.

Farrell, Chris. *Purpose and a Paycheck*. New York: Harper Collins Leadership, 2019.

Gaisford, Casandra. *Mid-Life Career Rescue: How to Confidently Leave a Job You Had and Start Living the Life You Love, Before It's Too Late*. Sante Fe: Blue Giraffe Press, 2019.

Gratton, Lynda. *Redesigning Work: How to Transform Your Organization & Make Hybrid Work for Everyone*. Cambridge, MA: The MIT Press, 2022.

Gratton, Lynda, and Andrew Scott. *The 100-Year Life: Living and Working in an Age of Longevity*. London: Bloomsbury Publishing, 2020.

Huth, Diane. *Reinvent Your Career: Beat Age Discrimination to Land Your Dream Job*. San Antonio: ISLA Publishing Group, 2018.

Milivinti, Alice, and David Rehkopf. "A New Map of Life: Work." Stanford Center on Longevity, May 24, 2021. https://longevity.stanford.edu/the-new-map-of-life-report/#1637124315004-b149a6e6-23ec.

Sedlar, Jeri, and Rick Miners. *Don't Retire, Rewire!: 5 Steps to Fulfilling Work that fuels your passion, suits your personality, fills your pocket*. New York: Alpha Books, 2018.

Sonsino, Yvonne. *The New Rules of Living Longer: How to Survive Your Longer Life*. London: MSL Publishing, 2015.

## Values, Financial Planning, and Mid-Life

Bachrach, Bill. *Values-Based Financial Planning*. San Diego: Aim High Publishing, 2000.

Barrett, Richard. *Everything I Have Learned About Values*. Durham, NC: Lulu Publishing Services, 2018. https://longevity.stanford.edu/the-new-map-of-life-report/#1637124315004-b149a6e6-23ec.

Find a CFP Professional: Let's Make a Plan. https://www.letsmakeaplan.org.

Potgieter, Kim. *Midlife Money Makeover*. Cape Town: Tafelberg, 2021.

Streeter, Jialu Liu. "New Map of Life Domain Report—Financial Security." April 2021, Final Version.

## Habits for Healthy Longevity

Buettner, Dan. *The Blue Zones Challenge: A 4-Week Plan for a Longer, Better Life*. Washington, D.C.: National Geographic, 2021.

Buettner, Dan. *The Blue Zones Kitchen: 100 Recipes to Live to 100*. Washington, D.C.: National Geographic, 2019.

Dienstmann, Giovanni. *Practical Meditation: A Simple Step-by-Step Guide*. New York: D.K. Publishing, 2018.

Esmonde-White, Miranda. *Aging Backwards: Reverse the Aging Process and Look 10 Years Younger in 30 Minutes a Day*. New York: Harper Wave, 2018.

Gundry, Steven R. *The Longevity Paradox: How to Die Young at a Ripe Old Age*. New York: Harper Wave, 2019.

Kabat-Zinn, Jon. *Wherever You Go There You Are: Mindfulness Meditation in Everyday Life*. New York: Hatchette, 2005.

Kross, Ethan. *Chatter: The Voice in Our Head, Why It Matters, and How to Harness It*. New York: Crown, 2021.

Longo, Valter. *The Longevity Diet: Discover the New Science Behind Stem Cell Activation and Regeneration to Slow Aging, Fight Disease, and Optimize Weight*. New York: Avery, 2018.

Roizen, Michael F., Peter Linneman, and Albert Ratner. *The Great Age Reboot: Cracking the Longevity Code for a Younger Tomorrow*. Washington, D.C.: National Geographic, 2022.

Schatzker, Mark. *The End of Craving: Recovering the Lost Wisdom of Eating Well*. New York: Avid Reader Press, 2021.

Walker, Matthew. *Why We Sleep: Unlocking the Power of Sleep and Dreams*. New York: Scribner, 2017.

## Intergenerational Relationships

Freedman, Marc. *How to Live Forever: The Enduring Power of Connecting the Generations*. New York: Public Affairs, 2018.

Gambone, James V. *Together for Tomorrow: Building Community Through Intergenerational Dialogue*, Crystal Bay, MN: Elder Eye Press, 2020.

Eldera.ai https://www.eldera.ai/.

Encore.org https://encore.org/.

Johfre, Sasha Shen. "Report on Intergenerational Relationships." Stanford Center on Longevity's New Map of Life Program, August 2021. https://longevity.stanford.edu/the-new-map-of-life-report/#1637124315004-b149a6e6-23ec.

## Social Life in Later Life

Hartford Funds. "The Social Portfolio: Why friendships are so important to aging well." https://www.hartfordfunds.com/insights/investor-insight/mit/the-social-portfolio.html.

Joseph Coughlin. *The Social Portfolio*. Hartford Funds. June 15, 2022. https://www.hartfordfunds.com/insights/investor-insight/mit/the-social-portfolio/the-social-portfolio.html.

## Planning for Help Before You Need It

Gambone, James V. *ReFire® Your Life! A guide for those who can't retire—or don't want to*, Crystal Bay, MN: Elder Eye Press, 2011.

Gambone, James V., and Rhonda Travland. *Who Says Men Don't Care? A Man's Guide to Balanced and Guilt-Free Caregiving*. CreateSpace Independent Publishing Platform, 2011.

Leider, Richard J. *The Power of Purpose with Richard Leider*, St. Paul, Minnesota, Twin Cities Public Television recorded broadcast.

MIT AgeLab. "Caregiving and Well-Being." https://agelab.mit.edu/caregiving-and-well-being/overview.

Logeland, Denise. *10 Things Every Family Should Know: Aging with Dignity and Independence*, St. Paul, Minnesota. Twin Cities Public Television e-book, 2015.

National Academies of Sciences, Engineering, and Medicine 2020. *Social Isolation and Loneliness in Older Adults: Opportunities for the Health Care System*. Washington, DC: The National Academies Press, 2020. https://doi.org/10.17226/25663.

Stum, Marlene. *Identifying Financial Security Goals for Later Life*, University of Minnesota Twin Cities, College of Education and Human Development, web page, worksheet and online quiz https://extension.umn.edu/personal-finances/identifying-financial-security-goals-later-life.

## End of Life/Legacy

Baines, Barry. *The Ethical Will Writing Guide Workbook*. Minneapolis: Josaba Limited, 2001.

Compassion & Choices. *My End-of-Life Decisions: An Advance Planning Guide and Toolkit*. https://compassionandchoices.org/resources/my-end-of-life-decisions-an-advance-planning-guide-and-toolkit.

Cullen, Melanie, and Shea Irving, *Get It Together: Organize Your Records So Your Family Won't Have To*. Ninth Edition. Berkeley, CA: NOLO, 2020.

Hudson, Terrie Davoll. *Leave a Legacy that Counts: create one at any age*. Alpharetta, GA: BookLogix, 2019.

Lee, Barbara Coombs. *Finish Strong: Putting Your Priorities First at Life's End*. Littleton, CO: Compassion & Choices, 2019.

Roser, Laura A. *Your Meaning Legacy: How to Cultivate & Pass on Non-Financial Assets*. Solana Beach, CA: Golden Legacy Press, 2018.

Stum, Marlene. *Who Gets Grandma's Yellow Pie Plate: A Guide for Passing on Personal Possessions*. Minneapolis: University of Minnesota Extension Service, 2011.

Taylor, Daniel. *Creating a Spiritual Legacy: How to Share Your Stories, Values, and Wisdom*. Grand Rapids, MI: Brazos Press, 2011.

Susan B. Turnbull. *The Wealth of Your Life: A Step-by-Step Guide for Creating Your Ethical Will*. Fourth Edition. Manchester-by-the-Sea, MA: Benedict Press, 2017.

## Wisdom

Bateson, Mary Catherine. *Composing a Further Life: The Age of Active Wisdom*. New York: Vintage Books, 2010.

Conley, Chip. *Wisdom@Work: The Making of a Modern Elder*. New York: Currency, 2018.

Jeste, Dilip and Scott Lafee. *Wiser: The Scientific Roots of Wisdom, Compassion, and What Makes Us Good*. Louisville, CO: Sounds True Press, 2020.

Jeste-Thomas Wisdom Index. [A free resource to assess your wisdom.] https://medschool.ucsd.edu/research/aging/research/Pages/SD-WISE.aspx.

Modern Elder Academy. https://www.modernelderacademy.com/.

## Goal-Setting

Dienstmann, Giovanni. *Mindful Self-Discipline: Living With Purpose and Achieving Your Goals in a World of Distractions*. LiveAndDare Publications, 2021.

Rohn, Jim. *The Jim Rohn Guide to Goal Setting*. Lake Dallas, TX: Success, 2014.

Rohn, Jim. Goal-Setting Workshop on Youtube, Part 1. https://www.youtube.com/watch?v=CO7ybUb1n7o.

Rohn, Jim. Goal-Setting Workshop on Youtube, Part 2. https://www.youtube.com/watch?v=xJSMvolr3XU.

Rohn, Jim. Goal-Setting Workshop, Part 3. https://www.youtube.com/watch?v=tJ1VQ0Ac0PU&t=794s.

Tracy, Brian. *Goals! How to Get Everything You Want—Faster Than You Ever Thought Possible*. Second Edition. San Francisco: Berrett-Koehler Publishers, 2010.

## Other Research on Aging and Resources

Age Wave. https://agewave.com.

AARP. https://www.aarp.org/.

Milken Institute Center for the Future of Aging. https://milkeninstitute.org/centers/center-for-the-future-of-aging.

MIT Agelab. https://agelab.mit.edu/.

Standford Center on Longevity. https://longevity.stanford.edu/.

# Notes

## A Note to Clients

1   *Longevity and the New Journey of Retirement, An Edward Jones and Age Wave Study*, 2022, 4. https://www.edwardjones.com/us-en/media/27386.

## Chapter 1: Moving from Retirement Planning to Longevity Planning

2   *Money*, November 2018, 42–43.

3   *Money*, 43.

4   KVUE TV, https://www.kvue.com/article/news/local/103-year-old-georgetown-man-attempts-world-record-tandem-skydive/269-3f26f4b4-4a47-4b7d-8d09-356d329065bf.

5   American Federation for Aging Research, https://www.afar.org/what-is-geroscience.

6   The Buck Institute website, https://www.buckinstitute.org/.

7   Nir Barzilai, *Age Later: Health Span, Life Span, and the New Science of Longevity* (New York: St. Martin's Press, 2020), inside the front jacket cover.

8   Barzilai, 246.

9   Barzilai, 147.

10  Barzilai, 148.

11  Robin Seaton Jefferson, *Forbes*, August 26, 2019, 04:54 EDT, "'Extraordinary' Breakthroughs in Anti-Aging Research Will 'Happen Faster Than People Think,'" https://www.forbes.com/sites/robinseatonjefferson/2019/08/26/how-extraordinary-breakthroughs-in-anti-aging-research-will-happen-faster-than-people-think/?sh=3bc938e233dd.

12  Michael Roizen, M.D., "Be Half the Age You Are by 2030," Global Wellness Summit, April 21, 2021. https://www.youtube.com/watch?v=O0pLxy2NUKs&t=1999s.

13  Lynda Gratton and Andrew Scott, *The 100-Year Life: Living and Working in the Age of Longevity* (London: Bloomsbury, 2020), 32.

14  Lynda Gratton, Barclays Beyond 100 Video, https://privatebank.barclays.com/non-ppc-campaign/see-beyond/.

15  Gratton, Barclays Beyond 100.

16  Paul H. Irving, *The Upside of Aging: How Long Life is Changing the World of Health, Work, Innovation, Policy, and Purpose* (Hoboken, NJ: Wiley, 2014), xxi.

17  Richard J. Leider and David A. Shapiro, *Who Do You Want to Be When You Grow Old?: The Path to Purposeful Aging* (Oakland: Barrett-Koehler Publishers, 2021), inside the front jacket cover.

18  Lance Secretan, *The Spark, the Flame, and the Torch: Inspire Self. Inspire Others. Inspire the World* (Caledon, ONT: The Secretan Center, 2010), 33.

19  Sectretan, 19.

20  Cassandra Gaisford, *Mid-life Career Rescue: The Call for Change 2020* (Santa Fe: Blue Giraffe Publishing, 2019), xii.

21  Gaisford, 203.

## Chapter 2: Understanding Juvenescence for Your Longevity Journey

22  Charlton T. Lewis, *A Latin Dictionary* (Oxford: Oxford University Press, 1980), 1020.

23  Robert Pogue Harrison, *Juvenescence: A Cultural History of Our Age* (Chicago: University of Chicago Press, 2014), x.

24  Jim Mellon and Al Chalabi, *Juvenescence: Investing in the Age of Longevity* (Fruitful Publications: Isle of Man, UK, 2017), 282.

25  Lynda Gratton and Andrew Scott, *The 100-Year Life: Living and Working in an Age of Longevity* (London: Bloomsbury Publishing, 2020), 201.

26  Mercer's Redesigning later life, 2019, https://www.mercer.com/content/dam/mercer/attachments/private/gl-2020-6010715-mn-next-age-redesigning-later-life-mercer.pdf.

27  Gratton and Scott, 223.

## Chapter 3: Identifying Core Values for Longevity Planning

28  Ed Diener and Robert Biswas-Diener, *Happiness: Unlocking the Mysteries of Psychological Wealth* (Malden, MA: Blackwell Publishing, 2008), 216.

## Chapter 4: Adopting and Enhancing Habits for Healthy Longevity

29  Sophie Haslett, DailyMail.com, January 27, 2020, https://www.dailymail.co.uk/femail/article-7936339/Everything-need-know-Blue-Zones-Diet-make-slim.html.

30  Miranda Esmonde-White, *Aging Backwards* (New York: HarperCollins Publishers, 2018), inside the front jacket cover. See also Chapter 4, "Meet Your Muscles, Ligaments, Joints, and Fascia," 45–65.

31  Thorn Rieck, "10,000 steps a day: Too low? Too High?" Mayoclinic.org, https://www.mayoclinic.org/healthy-lifestyle/fitness/in-depth/10000-steps/art-20317391#:~:text=The%20average%20American%20walks%20 3%2C000,a%20day%20every%20two%20weeks.

32  Mayo Clinic Staff, "Aerobic Exercise," Mayoclinc.org., https://www.mayoclinic.org/healthy-lifestyle/fitness/basics/aerobic-exercise/hlv-20049447.

33  ACSM Guidelines for Strength Training, https://www.acsm.org/all-blog-posts/certification-blog/acsm-certified-blog/2019/07/31/acsm-guidelines-for-strength-training-featured-download.

34  Gabriela Miranda, *USA Today*, November 9, 2021, https://www.usatoday.com/story/news/health/2021/11/09/whats-best-time-fall-asleep-your-heart-and-why/6350265001/.

35  Johns Hopkins Medicine, https://www.hopkinsmedicine.org/health/wellness-and-prevention/a-day-that-leads-to-your-best-nights-sleep.

36  Roizen, Global Wellness Summit 2021.

37  James V. Gambone, Ph.D., *ReFire® Your Life! A Guide for Those Who Can't Retire—Or Don't Want To* (Crystal Bay, MN: Elder Eye Press, 2011), 67.

38  Mayo Clinic website, https://www.mayoclinic.org/healthy-lifestyle/stress-management/in-depth/stress-relief/art-20044456.

39  Daniel J. Levitin, *Successful Aging: A Neuroscientist Explores the Power and Potential of Our Lives* (New York: Dutton, 2020), 398.

40  Levitin, 365.

41  Levitin, 401.

42  "One minute Meditation," youtube.com https://www.youtube.com/watch?v=F7PxEy5IyV4.

43  "Mindfulness Meditation – Quick 15 Min Stress Relief Version" youtube.com.  https://www.youtube.com/watch?v=8v45WSuAeYI.

## Chapter 5: Building Intergenerational Relationships

44  Eldera.ai https://www.eldera.ai/.

45  Eldera.

46  Marc Freedman, *How to Live Forever: The Enduring Power of Connecting the Generations* (New York: Public Affairs, 2018), 97.

47  Freedman, 134.

48  Paul Irving, "The Villages is a retirement 'paradise'---so why is that a problem?" Marketwatch.com, September 21, 2021, https://www.marketwatch.com/story/the-villages-is-a-retirement-paradiseso-why-is-that-a-problem-11631818529.

49 Freedman, 141.

50 James V. Gambone, *Together for Tomorrow: Building Community Through Intergenerational Dialogue* (Crystal Bay, MN: Elder Eye Press, 2020).

## Chapter 6: Planning for Help Before You Need It

51 Stum, M. "Identifying Later Life Financial Goals Worksheet." University of Minnesota Extension, St. Paul, 2022. https://extension.umn.edu/later-life-decision-making/identifying-financial-security-goals-later-life.

52 National Academies of Sciences, Engineering, and Medicine 2020. *Social Isolation and Loneliness in Older Adults: Opportunities for the Health Care System.* Washington, DC: The National Academies Press. https://doi.org/10.17226/25663.

53 Nicholas R. Nicholson, "A Review of Social Isolation: An Important but Understated Condition in Older Adults," Springer Science+Business Media, online, 6 July 2012.

## Chapter 7: Leaving a Holistic Personal Legacy

54 Daniel Taylor, *Creating a Spiritual Legacy: How to Share Your Stories, Values, and Wisdom* (Grand Rapids, MI: Brazos Press, 2011), xi.

55 Stephen R. Covey, *The 7 Habits of Highly Effective People* (New York: Fireside, 1989), 96--97.

56 See Marlene S. Stum, *Who Gets Grandma's Yellow Pie Plate? Workbook: A Guide to Passing on Personal Possessions* (Minneapolis: University of Minnesota Extension Service, 2011).

57 Barry K. Baines, *The Ethical Will Writing Guide Workbook* (Minneapolis: Josaba Limited, 2001), 1.

58 Banes,1.

## Chapter 8: Mining Wisdom for Balanced Goal Setting

59 Levitan, 27.

60 Brad Jenson, "The Wisdom Quadrants: A Dynamic Model of Holistic Wisdom," Modern Elder Academy Wisdom Well, March 19, 2022. https://wisdomwell.modernelderacademy.com/the-wisdom-quadrants-a-dynamic-model-of-holistic-wisdom.

61 Dilip Jeste and Scott LaFee, *Wiser: The Scientific Roots of Wisdom, Compassion, and What Makes Us Good* (Boulder, CO: Sounds True, 2020), 5.

62 Oishi, S., & Westgate, E.C. August 12, 2021. "A Psychologically Rich Life: Beyond Happiness and Meaning." Psychological Review. Advance online publication. http://dx.doi.org/10.1037/rev0000317.

63  Oishi and Westgate.

64  Jim Rohn's Goal's Workshop, Part 1 https://www.youtube.com/
    watch?v=CO7ybUb1n7o&t=7s.

65  Joseph F. Coughlin, Ph.D., "Three Questions That Can Predict Future
    Quality of Life," MIT AgeLab and Hartford Funds. https://www.
    hartfordfunds.com/dam/en/docs/pub/prospectingmaterials/Whitepapers/
    MF929.

# Disclosures

The information contained in this book does not purport to be a complete description of the securities, markets, or developments referred to in this material. The information has been obtained from sources considered to be reliable, but we do not guarantee that the foregoing material is accurate or complete. Any information is not a complete summary or statement of all available data necessary for making an investment decision and does not constitute a recommendation. Any opinions of the chapter authors are those of the chapter author and not necessarily those of RJFS or Raymond James. Expressions of opinion are as of the initial book publishing date and are subject to change without notice.

Raymond James Financial Services, Inc. is not responsible for the consequences of any particular transaction or investment decision based on the content of this book. All financial, retirement and estate planning should be individualized as each person's situation is unique.

This information is not intended as a solicitation or an offer to buy or sell any security referred to herein. Keep in mind that there is no assurance that our recommendations or strategies will ultimately be successful or profitable nor protect against a loss. There may also be the potential for missed growth opportunities that may occur after the sale of an investment. Recommendations, specific investments or strategies discussed may not be suitable for all investors. Past performance may not be indicative of future results. You should discuss any tax or legal matters with the appropriate professional.

Made in United States
Cleveland, OH
26 March 2025

15511827R10105